What people are sayi

Kristi's story is not much different than many of ours. We all have the "shit that has happened" and we can choose to be victim or warrior. Kristi takes real life through her own stories that are so heartfelt it's easy to relate to, and teaches us how we have a choice to rise up or stay down. In 15 years, I have not read a book from cover to cover until this one. It is a true love story—the kind that makes you want to love yourself more for all of the realness life throws at you.

Becky Schoenig—St. Louis, MO
Co-owner of SymBowl—a healthy lifestyle conscious restaurant
A Spiritual Coach

Vulnerability and sharing our truth is contagious. In Coming Home: A Love Story, *Kristi Peck shows she is a powerful spiritual teacher articulating her journey so beautifully. Celebrating her life's experiences, she will inspire you to own your powers and welcome your true self along the way. This book is a very easy read that resonated with me deeply, while taking me to a new level of savoring the moments in my life.*

Stacy Sullivan—St. Louis, MO
Owner, Sol Sweat

Kristi Peck is a true gift in how she listens, empowers and loves. Coming Home: A Love Story *is as inspiring as Kristi is in person. Her stories will challenge you to think about your own life and truth in order to become the best version of you in your present, which is the only place we live. Kristi's ideas about love, letting go and standing in your own truth will center you today. And she does it all with a smile and a hug. Read this book and then...LIVE it.*

Pam Wilson, MSW, LCSW
Senior Editor, Davis Creative
Blogger at: youcallitchaosicallitlife.wordpress.com
Free-lance writer, creator of *Write ON!*
Author, *S.O.S. From Suburbia*

coming
HOME

A LOVE STORY

AWAKEN YOUR TRUTH

Kristi Peck

Coming Home: A Love Story
Awaken Your Truth
Kristi Peck
XO Publishing

Published by XO Publishing, St. Louis, MO
Copyright ©2018 Kristi Peck
All rights reserved.

Editor: Cathy Marshall
Cover and Interior design: Davis Creative, DavisCreative.com

Library of Congress Cataloging-in-Publication Data
Library of Congress Control Number: 2018902912
Kristi Peck
Coming Home: A Love Story, Awaken Your Truth
ISBN: 978-1-7320924-0-2
Library of Congress subject headings:
1. SEL032000 - Self-help/Spiritual Life
2. OCC019000 - Mind,Body,Spirit/Inspiration and Personal Growth
3. FAM034000 - Family & Relationships/Parenting

2018

All my love......

To EVERY SINGLE teacher in my life—
my husband, my children, my family, my friends;
the people I have worked with, taught and supported;
the acquaintances who have touched my heart;
and the many experiences that have awakened me to
the unlimited capacity in each of us. I believe in the human spirit.
I believe in organic wisdom and "home baked" wisdom.
We learn from our own life what we need, what we want,
what brings out the best for us, what does not serve us well,
what pushes us forward, and what holds us back.
I am a learner.

For all of my teachers...a wholehearted THANK YOU
for the lessons, the love, and the freedom of surrender.

XOXO to You!!

Inspired from the beginning

God has always been important to me. Most of the time, I am not really sure what that means. I have found throughout my life, a curiosity taking hostage my thinking and attempting warfare with the question—who is God?

In this story—my story—God is meant to be symbolic of an entity of love. Feel free to make the God in my story one of your own understanding. Quite often, I even use other names as I refer to a power bigger than all of us together. This higher power, a force of love, could be Buddha, the Universe, nature, Jesus, the Holy Spirit, Mother Mary, etc.

I have a highly intuitive style when writing and in my work. This power source allows me to connect to an emotional depth needed to support growth, learning, and a higher consciousness. In my writing, this source is influential in bringing a deeper element of understanding to the story.

—

Driving home one day, the song "Arms" by Christina Perri grabbed my heart with such fierceness that I knew it must be calling on me.

I listened over and over again to its lyrics. It made sense and it was confusing. My heart was demanding an understanding.

I had always known that I am a duality of two parts united in love. These two must collaborate to obtain a life lived well—happy, healthy, and joyful. One often seen as negative, contradictory, and utterly obsessed with pulling apart, and the other sweet and innocent comprised of a pureness and a loyalty. Like the chambers within the beating heart of our human-ness, the consciousness of this duality had awakened a movement within me some time before. The ego controlling my every move and thought pattern. My soul crying desperately to be seen, to be heard, and to be acknowledged. This awakening was a strong force like the morning after a fierce storm of such. I knew I could not look back. I would not go back. I could only go forward and gain the power already within me, and truthfully wake up to who I am.

The language of this song was intense and rumbled within those chambers of my beating heart.

I did not get it at first. What was this song telling me?

"I never thought that You would be the one to hold my heart."

Wow! That feels like the real deal. A true love between two totally separate and totally united. Is that my heart speaking? Who is it speaking to? Is it to my ego?

I thought the heart and the ego were not compatible. I was brought up to believe the ego was a negative source to be reckoned with in many situations. It craves control and toxic idealism. It doubts the slightest bit of wholesomeness.

I listened some more.

"You put your arms around me and I'm home."

What is this home the song is speaking of? Could it be an external place to go? Could something external really feel safe like a home?

No. It must be an inner habitation.

Yes. But where is the safest place within me?

My heart leaped forward in that moment in response to my inquiry. And I knew.

And within that same moment of exaltation of joy was a rainstorm of sadness mixed with tears.

"The world is coming down on me and I can't find a reason to be loved."

Oh my! Do I really feel that way?

Yes. Deep within the walls of my silent retreat, was an unworthiness.

⟶

And so my journey began with me, all of me, paying attention.

⟶

It was a rough time managed by quiet moments of tears and fears. My insides were like mini roller coasters intertwined and moving at a speed unknown before.

I would find solitude and stillness in my walks. Losing myself in the arms of music became a daily antecedent to the grind of uncharted territory.

"You just thought this would never happen to you," he said to me, and he was dead on.

Between my educational knowledge and the mix of wise experiences as a teacher and a babysitter—as well as my own instinct—I wholeheartedly believed the way to parent was exactly as we had been doing every day since their birth. So, when Son began to live in a constant state of anger, mouthing responses to us, his parents, that were not only unkind but downright unbelievable, we entered our stormy season as a family. The solitude and stilling walks were the location of my inner peace. It was a breath of fresh air to the whaling motion of the disturbance that seemed to be enveloping our existence.

It was on one such walk that love showed up in the most miraculous way.

Mesmerized by the chatter in my mind and moving quickly upon the sidewalk, I was suddenly stopped by a force that held me in place. My head shifted to a downward momentum. In this split second, a familiar figure caught my mind's eye and captured my attention. The sidewalk was carved out and emptied in the outline of a heart. It held me captive as I glared into the knowing. This heart felt warm as I gazed upon its beauty. A smile crept upon my face, and I instantly found myself walking on.

A shift into perspective had occurred in the most present of all moments that day. A swelling of strength and courage unfolded from the mystic corners of an unrecognizable place within me. I felt I could handle the stormy season I was in and, most importantly, I knew I was in the storm for a purpose grander than my mind's intellect.

From that precise moment, the hearts began showing up pretty regularly. At first I thought what a strange coincidence. I now know, there are no coincidences in this world we live in. The Universe works with each of us to guide us toward the life we are meant to live, dropping faith, hope, and love exactly when we need a dose of encouragement. The heart marks were my North Star to light my way and whisper so lovingly that "in the present moment" was the exact right spot for me to be. Eckhart Tolle describes this awareness as "intensely conscious of the present moment."

The hearts always showed up when I was with family or in moments of deep thought about my many roles as a parent, a friend, a family member, a teacher, and a human. They appeared in the right place for me to see them, and there was always such comfort that came from them. I finally began to photograph them as the anecdotal evidence of these heart marks.

To this day, I find the heart marks in moments I release to God and the Angels. The hearts reassure me they have my back and I am loved. They are gentle hugs when I find myself feeling nervous or anxious. They bring me joy. Each time one appears, I smile, I thank, and I surrender to a power bigger than myself. This power has my life in the palm of a lovingness AND, in these present moments, I am in a joy-filled awe for all that life is, can be, and will be.

A Course in Miracles explains our goal is not to seek love but to remove our blocks to the awareness that love already exists.

The heart marks were life-changing and life-building. They were miracles of love.

Each experience within my story brought a heart mark within it. They were my constant, reassuring me that all was well and I was exactly where I needed to be. Upon their discovery, I instantly shifted perspective, opened my heart more, and surrendered to God.

My hope for you is that you can unblock love and experience the love that God, the Angels, and the Universe want for you. You are love! Open up to that awareness, and believe love is always a real possibility.

Introduction

My home is where the heart is.
—Erasure "Blue Savannah"

I searched for years to find solace in my own skin.

I met people who were heartwarming, and in an instant, I'd chum up and radically think we were besties. Many of those relationships would snap out in a split second as the reflection soon told me loud and clear, "This is not your place to be." Saddened and broken apart, I would slump around, inching my way through the days searching once again for home.

Events would swirl me into their energy, and I would find myself completely enthralled with the learning left behind, once again searching for home.

It wasn't until I splattered in pieces, frozen in my own skin and unable to breathe through the moments, that I knew the only way out was to conduct a search and rescue for my heart. The work was hard. My own wholeheartedness saved my life, AND I am forever grateful to that frozen moment in time.

The inspiration that breathed life back into my life were tiny spar-kles of loving instants that opened my eyes to seeing in a new format, unblocked my ears to hearing the silence, and slowly dis-lodged the heart that had been stuck in fear, anxiety, and uncom-fortable existence. Finding my life through the insides of my own soul and the re-beating of my own heart was like breaking a chain link with only your hands. Clearing the clutter from the cobwebs of my life experiences gave me the space to find the inspiration to live well, to align every decision with my soul's dream, and to maximize the little daily instances that matter more than we think they do.

Home is not the fancy brick palace filled with all the niceties that money can buy. Home is the everyday beating of your choices, your actions, and your love as you align the spiral colors of a well-lived life. Home is the joyful existence of your heart. Home is where the heart is, and only there will you find peace and love.

◠

My day.

The one decided for me to enter the world…this world…the world I would inhabit as my own came as my mother sat in church. Yes! It was a church day that I decided (or someone else decided for me for that matter) to enter this world. And, to top it off, my name means follower of Christ.

So, it would seem reasonable that my comfort has come from God, Jesus, the Holy Spirit, Angels and Archangels. I have always found comfort in the rhythmic verses of those wise words said often in liturgy. Great and all-powerful epiphanies have occurred to me while relaxing in church, in quiet places of worship, and during the service itself.

I have never thought of myself as a nature girl. Maybe because it was thrust upon me as a young child. Yet, I do find solace in quiet, still moments sitting in a park, walking on the beach, or journeying on a mountain.

One of my favorite verses landed in my lap, literally, on a trip into an Episcopal service. It comes at the end of the liturgy as we, the congregants, are about to depart the sacred space and walk back into our own lives. The verse reads –

> "Send us now into the world in peace, and grant us strength and courage to love you and serve you with gladness and singleness of heart."

Every time I read it, I am challenged to live well as a peace-full person, to live in service as I do my daily living, to be guided by the Holy Spirit with his strength and gentle en-courage-ment, and to be heart-centered every chance I get.

It is an invitation to awaken to the newest of possibilities each day and be graciously given that awakening at every moment. Living well is not about holding myself in high regard as one who makes no mistakes, lives in a perfection state of mind, or perpetually acts in ego. It is more about honoring the falls, the failures, and the errors in judgment as a way of life guided by a pure space of love within myself that knows.

That all-knowing is the one space that can be trusted. Going inward allows me to embrace that one dwelling where I can be me, and I can live freely. It is my home.

In *A Course in Miracles*, my home is God's home, and the Holy Spirit can always help me get there when I drift away.

> "The Holy Spirit recognizes it perfectly because it is his own dwelling place; the place in the mind where he is at home. You are at home there, too, because it is a place of peace, and peace is of God."

A Course in Miracles also states that our egoist moments, those that cause us separation from who we are, our most sacred selves, are "teaching devices for bringing you home."

These stories, my stories, were just that. They were teaching mechanisms for learning my identity. I came into this world as a loving being and along the way, I got distracted and out of alignment. It was no purposeful doing on anyone's part. These stories and the humans in them were fulfilling a purpose on my growth journey. They were brought into my life to unlock the door to my awakening and open my heart to love. There is no shame or blame for the result of each story. I fully honor the reality of each one and all it entailed as strategies for guiding me home.

And home is where the heart is.

The OPENING

"How strange that the nature of life is change, yet the nature of human beings is to resist change. And how ironic that the difficult times we fear might ruin us are the very ones that can break us open and help us blossom into who we were meant to be."
—Elizabeth Lesser

I had a moment that literally broke me open. It ripped away the residue of past fears and tightly hidden beliefs. The pain of the incident was the impetus for me consciously deciding to find out who I was and return to love.

blind-sided —
the unexpected gifting
of a situation
unknown to ever exist

The big classroom of life is open to each one of us once we embark upon our journey of self-discovery. Unexpected events or occurrences can launch you in a direction that warms your heart, yet not before it completely opens you up. If we are living well, our entire life is filled with growth endurances to hurdle and bring us safely into the next season. Change is hard, and when we sit with it for any period of time, our bodies react with a super-charged race between our feelings and our bodily actions. In this race, our feelings always win. Thus, we land in a perpetual state of avoidance for fear of what will come next and questioning if we are ready. We are never prepared for the most sacred openings of our heart. They are usually blind-sided experiences that gift us in ways never known to exist.

—◦—

The day my oldest was born, I vowed so many things to him. The one that always stuck with me was that I would NEVER do anything or say anything to make him feel small and unworthy. I had felt, from my own life experiences, the never-ending dismissal of me. The moment my son came into our world, all I could think about was, "How could a parent leave a child, not see a child, and not hear a child?"

AND that day I vowed never to do that. I vowed to love him, take care of him, and do all I could for him. Little did I know…those promises would haunt me on the day in October when my phone rang…he was calling…in trouble.

My life experiences gave me perceptive thoughts. Those thoughts cooked into my head, and eventually into my heart, creating a belief system. That belief system became my navigation system. Our brains are wired for systemic structure and thus it is easily a manipulation tactic for our thoughts to become revenues of actions. They determine how we view the events and happenings in our life. They fuel a force behind such daily actions and often reactions. This belief system assumes the totality of who we are. It polices us into a revolving cycle of motivation.

The birth day of my firstborn was such that day. My belief system governed my pledge to him. I wholeheartedly allowed the take-over of my mind, body, and spirit to the most precious act of love. The gift…the most divine of all gifts was entrusted to us. I was his parent, and with that role came the obligation that he would be seen, heard, and given a sense of belonging to himself. I, his mom, would only offer him worthiness, and not a thing could ever take that away. I would make sure of it.

⌒

I had just come from the hospital where my father-in-law was gravely ill. My husband and I had been running a crazy schedule back and forth taking care of the kids—there were four of them—and taking care of him, working our jobs, and meeting our commitments.

I heard his voice as I answered the call, "Hi mom, I need you to come pick me up at Walmart. I just got arrested."

In the initial aftermath, I thought he was joking, so I replied, "Are you kidding?"

Calmly and seriously, he answered, "No, I'm serious."

In that instant, I began to shake uncontrollably…something in me knew I was in over my head. There came a quiet voice within me like a flashlight guiding my way that said, "Call her."

I listened to that quiet voice and called that girl.

That girl was a friend who has been with me since fourth grade. She is one of my tribers who does not judge and only cares for me. I called and immediately began to dump the shit that was bubbling from the fire that had just ignited within me.

Fear…cuss words…doubt…worry…fear…cuss words…fear… anger…cuss words…fear. It was the longest 14-minute drive and the most painful conversation.

The vows I made to him on that birthing day came hauntingly back to surface. I knew this was a BIG moment. I had only one chance to do this right, to see him, to hear him, to not leave him, and to make him feel worthy amidst a big mistake.

I remember as my friend hung up, she asked me, "What are you going to say?"

My voice wearily quivered as the words tumbled out—"I have no idea. I guess I'm just going to let go and hope God will tell me."

I entered the building while repeating in my head, "Help! I have no idea what to do. Help! Tell me what to do! Okay, I can do this! Oh, and thank you!"

Yep! The last words I said were, "Thank you!" I wasn't even sure if I believed the gratitude part. I knew in my heart that gratitude can change perspective. Letting go means throwing in the towel and saying, "Help me." The moment I walked into the office where they hold privacy moments, I looked at him and something immediately shifted in me. It was as if I was blanketed with calm and peace. I took a look at him and was wowed at what I saw—a smart, talented, hard-working, brilliant young man; a visionary, a wise one, a loving one, a kind one…my son—who happened to have made a mistake.

What was given to me was wisdom. Who he was did not change. What he did does not define who he is. Letting go means throwing all you think, all you believe, all you wanted out the door, and standing naked knowing you will be given all you need when it matters. The miracle that happened in that moment was an everyday miracle. When we come from a loving place within us…the miracles are there every day.

As we walked into our house that evening, I went straight to my room. I huddled on the bed, and I cried.

The thing about our ego is that it really wants to play the lead role in our life. It kept creeping in louder and louder as it laughed at me, and informed me, "See, you are not worthy. You are not a good parent like you thought. You are not good enough for this parenting thing."

And as I sat there it felt VERY familiar.

I flashed back to sitting on my bed the night my dad left us, when I cried tears of unworthiness (he couldn't stay for us), tears of fear (what is going to happen now—how are we going to do this), tears of shame (what will people think of us).

And in that scared moment on my bed with my son in the other room, I was enveloped with the same unworthiness, the same fear, and the same tears of shame. Thoughts scrambled in my head—"You thought you had this parenting thing. Ha! Foolish you are for that thinking. What kind of trouble will he get in to? And what will people think of us?"

The ego, as organizer, mandated more of these uncomfortable thoughts and feelings. And something else was a force working harder. When I let go, God was able to nudge his way into my heart. Part of me was softening to this mistake. Part of me was opening to my own un-comfort-able bubble.

I began to think and wonder, "What is going on with me? How is this about me?"

We had MANY talks over the next few days and weeks. In one of our talks, I asked him about the very things I was having a difficult time with.

"I know how people talk, aren't you worried about what they will say about you?" My fear kept on talking and asking, "I know who you are, but I am scared for what they will think of you."

His wise soul spoke comfortingly to me, "Mom, I do not give a shit what anybody thinks. I know who I am, and my friends know me, and that is all that matters."

I continued to inquire, "Aren't you scared of what will happen? What if you have to go to jail?"

The wisdom continued, "Mom, yeah maybe a little, but it'll be ok. I did what I did. I know it was not right what I did. I can't take it back. I just have to take the consequences and move on. I know I'll never do it again."

Those conversations happened days and weeks later. Silence is powerful. It is the freedom that everyone needs to find their way in all challenges.

What I remember most vividly in those days, weeks, and months following was an incessant mission to hold a loving space for him. I intently fixated on the joy he brought, the achievements he had obtained, and the inspiring qualities he had demonstrated. Daily I rehearsed the list of grateful tidings of his most authentic self.

In all the goodness I was frantically recalling, I could not forget the trudging path we had been on. There were equally many challenging times with him.

He was on a roller coaster of inconsistent choices from missing curfew, mouthy rudeness, and not-so-good grades to a willingness to help anyone, attend a mission trip with our church, and be fun to hang out with. His choices were nothing less than adolescent growing pains. Not one of his actions stood out to preach a message of trouble or discontent.

In one of my many walks of solitude, I looked up in search of answers to my waterfall of questions and concerns. The sky was blue and the whole world seemed to be shining bright. One lonely white cloud burst out at me…in the shape of a heart. That heart mark confirmed to me, in my tiny moment of agony, all was well.

God sends these miracle moments as well as earth angels to do and say exactly what needs to be seen and heard. Any time I needed the reassurance that all would be okay, God sent a friend, a coworker, and sometimes even a stranger to remind me of who he was.

One day I was getting the mail, and my neighbor stopped me. She said, "Hey, I have been wanting to tell you what a hard worker your son is. I haven't had a chance to tell you that. This summer he took such good care of my yard and was so responsible. You've done well."

She offered breath to me in a moment when I was having trouble finding my airways.

Another time, we were at school conferences, and a teacher shared an amazing anecdote of Son participating with valuable wisdom and insight regarding a character in a story. The teacher was in awe of Son's depth into the character. That teacher aided in my dis-ease with our present moment.

Those were God's loving miracles. They happened all the time and in the exact right moment to help me breathe, calm my nerves, and shift me from thinking with ego to my loving heart-space.

When you are under age and caught breaking the law, the community offers a restitution service as a way of counseling a family. We were scheduled to go before this court-appointed group, and as we drove to the meeting I encouraged Son to be himself and always uphold the truth.

Once again, I was shattered into a million pieces as we sat face-to-face with fear, with anger, and with openness. As Son vividly described his fun, his choices, and his behaviors, I was secretly crumbling and frantically begging God to stop time. There were aspects of that meeting that I literally thought a force was strangling me. Air would not, or maybe could not, get to my lungs. It was a moment of mixed emotions, and all of us in attendance were skirting around clothed in our own emotional MY-ne field. Son was brutally honest, and as a mother, I was both proud and mortified.

In the moments of being chastised for parenting with love, we were spat at for "allowing him to drink, to attend parties, and to make the choices he had made."

I caught myself violently shifting my body toward the other side of the table as I pleaded our way of parenting, "He is his own person. I have no control over what he chooses when he leaves our physical home."

That was not a working comment because it did little to shift the badgering that continued. Fear has a way of constructing stories and knowledge. These court-appointed persons were filled with fear, and my body began to shake uncontrollably once again knowing I was in over my head.

～◦

That challenge broke me…open. It forced me to face my own fears and inner dialogues. AND I am, to this day, so unbelievably grateful for it. What has evolved is a much stronger individual in each of us. The beauty of loving conversations, a deeper understanding of who we are, and a rock-solid foundation in knowing we are cared for from a power larger than life.

I knew I had to allow myself to sit with my pain and agony, feeling helpless from a loved one's decisions that had no attachment to me. Pain often results from the rising of an unforeseen circumstance. When this type of ambiguity occurs, it causes our humanness to desire a release immediately.

In Jill Bolte Taylor's book, *My Stroke of Insight*, about her recovery from a massive stroke, she explains the psychological mechanics of an emotion taking 90 seconds to run its course within our physical bodies. She describes the process of a chemical reaction to the emotion flowing through the body. If all goes well, the emotion will be over.

Pema Chodron, an American Tibetan Buddhist, confirms Taylor's insight, yet also converses a much different scenario. According to Chodron and Taylor, if we sit with pain and discomfort for 90 seconds with no judging, the feeling and the emotion (which are fluid channels of energy) will move through us like a tornado moves through a town in the springtime. Chodron adds, as humans, we often do not allow the emotion to run its full course through our physical bodies without judging it. This contributes to an instantaneous release channeling a stream of unconsciousness to conclude a script. These scripts become a chosen lifeline to our own suffering.

My physical workout occurred, almost daily. Some days I allowed the rainbow of emotions to jog through my boney structure, and others were completely clouded with the unconscious choice to story tell. I pried open the Pandora's box filled with insecurities, unworthiness, and lack of trust. My hiding could no longer occur in faith. God was forcing me to come clean. The story telling had to be rewritten.

Our kids are our grandest teachers. Son was teaching me to heal and helping me to trust and know my worth. In this broken moment, he air pumped me back to life. As difficult as this experience was for both of us, we grew up together during those months. I learned to trust me. I learned my worthiness. I learned my insecurities were always just opportunities to grow, not stop living life. I learned I do matter.

When Son got in trouble, my unworthy Self beliefs surfaced. In those moments when they bubbled over into my world, I really had only two options:

1. Shove them down and deflect the agony of each of them by making the incident all about him, which would result in his shaming, his fear-based thinking and living, and his inner voice being switched to another channel.

OR

2. Deal with them.

We all have the power of a warrior within us.

Think about it.

When any challenge arises, we can either fight it outside of our Self or come home to our Self. Arming ourselves to fight the battle on the outside makes us look like a warrior. These are things like snarky words, judgment about another, mean and hateful actions, numbing devices, and running away. Believe me, there is some power in these warrior-like tendencies, yet only in the short term. Another approach, often under-considered, is to open up to these painful emotions and feel them on the inside. Befriending our emotions when they arise is the true armor of a warrior and the only way to fight our battle in love. The real power of a warrior is that of going inward—sitting with our emotions, finding stillness and allowing the pain to move through us, honoring the emotions as they move through us, releasing judgement, and letting go of guilt for feeling.

I chose to go inward and boy, what a battle it was to fight. Going inward meant finding the quiet so I could actually hear what was being given to me by my loving divine guidance. Going inward meant taking care of me. I had lost that along the way on my journey with parenting and with life's roller coaster ride. Going inward meant getting rid of distractions—the outer world is loud. Going inward meant finding my answers to why—"Why was I feeling this way? Why was this bothering me? Why was I in fear? What was I scared of? Why was I not choosing love in this moment?"

A Course in Miracles says, "Whatever is missing in any relationship is that which you are not giving."

I worked diligently to get back to love within these everyday challenges of child-rearing. This opening was a double-duty manifestation. It was for him, and it was for me. In those days leading up to our moment of truth, I had not been giving love to me.

This open door reconstructed who I was as a human and who we were together as parent and child. I had been so focused on the physical-ness of who I was and who we were. I took us hostage in an outer world filled with image, expectations, and unrealistic identities.

I created us to be THAT family, and my own creation led us to the suffocation of who we really were as individuals and with each other. The smallest of light can create such a vision for the endless supply of possibilities that one can draw from that light to see.

The very essence of God, of which I had pulled away in the early years of my life, was calling me back to his loving arms. What an oxymoron I was experiencing as I had distracted myself from pain and sheltered myself within a world of my own making that encompassed fear, doubt, unworthiness.

That day of Son's error in decision-making was my opening. It was my gift. It was pure love. Uncovering the layers to that love would require unleashing the monumental overload of belief systems, of experiences, of inner talking and blind vision. Love offers freedom, and in these early days with Son I was definitely more imprisoned than free. I learned that freedom is peaceful, joyful, and loving.

Freedom offers a will of choice and gifts us with expansiveness to a world of pure bliss. It is not too good to be true. It is just that we often humanly decide to not bear witness to this place. It is and always will be offered to us by God.

With a sledge hammer in one hand and my memories in the other, I set forth on a journey of self-discovery. This expedition would wind me in and out of various dwelling places until I could decon-struct the impression.

I set out on a mission.

⟋⟍

Who am I? Who is asking: My heart or my head.

I do not remember.

Then go to the beginning and find your way back home.

Phase 1:
the IMPRESSION

*"Don't pretend to be what you're not, instead,
pretend to what you want to be, it is not pretense,
it is a journey to self-realization."*
–Michael Bassey Johnson

The impressions were my beginning. They were my experiences in which I chose to believe something significant about myself. I will never forget them because they are etched into my heart as the scars that brought me to where I am today.

There are moments within one's lifetime that will occur without conscious thought. They can disrupt the natural tendencies to be oneself. They can appear silently or swoop in with a vengeance.

Impressions are moments of extreme pressure followed by a significant portrait of the occurrence. The pressure occurs when experiences are driven from a central point of emotions. The emotions override the reality, thereby causing a significant influence to be induced. This induction formulates an image which can be such that an alteration takes place. The portrait is a remembering of the pressure and the influence it left.

Such moments, to no fault of the players, can leave us not the same. They cause a distraction within our heart, and we find ourselves allowing them to stay. Forever implanted into our psyche, these impressions change the course of our life direction and become our most prized possessions.

The influence of such occurrences often go on without an understanding, until an earthly storm causes the surface of such beliefs to seep through the pores of our existence. It is in this defining moment of impact that we have a choice. We can sit with the burden of such falsities, or we can choose to allow the rumble, the pain, and the agony to pry us open to who we are in the depth of our soul.

our mirror —
how we see ourselves

It was a hot summer day. I was attending Vacation Bible School at a Methodist church in my hometown. At the age of eight, I knew I was loved. I grew up with a brother and a sister and many cousins. Holidays were fun as we laughed, ate good food, and celebrated. These rituals were important to me, and I valued the symbolic essence of them. VBS was another family ritual. Those half days for a week filled with the luxury of bible stories, crafts, and games with friends. And this hot day was like every other VBS day.

We headed outside for the traditional game of Red Rover. Secretly I hated that game. It would always freak me out to watch someone who desperately wanted to break our hands apart come charging with such fierceness. To me, it was scary! I think there were times I just let go. The decisive moment of choosing between getting hurt (because it would rip a ping of pain in your hand and fore-arms as they rushed through the tightly held grip!!) or letting go. I always chose letting go. Maybe at an early age, I intuitively knew letting go would always be the winning move.

Boy, do I remember how hot it was! I had a white T-shirt with red detailing on it, blue shorts, white bobby socks, and my Champion shoes. As we ran, I got hotter. My hair was not really cooperating on that day. It had become bushy and frizzy, and it was not quite long enough for a ponytail. I shoved it behind my ears and made a thermal decision to cool off.

As any creative would do, I took the middle of the front of my T-shirt and pulled it through the top of my shirt to create a halter.

21

Whoosh!!!! I instantly felt cooler. It worked, and I was thrilled with my fired-up solution and entered the game as a fierce competitor.

One moment I was laughing and giggling, and the next I was standing in front of my mother. Our eyes met as she undid my shirt in her hasty fashion and began intensely scolding me for wearing my shirt like that.

In my confused fog at the quickness of this moment, all I heard from her mouth was, "We don't wear clothes like that." "We don't show our bodies in public like that." "What were you thinking?"

These words felt harsh and somewhat unnecessary. I tried to open my mouth. Nothing exited. I looked at her hoping she would understand my confusion.

To no avail, I lost my way that day. When she walked away, I remember finding a spot on the ground. Tears surfaced in my eyes. I was hurt. I was embarrassed. I was confused.

And so the story began to unfold in my head. My body was not to be shown. My body was to be hidden. My body was not beautiful to show. This story unfolding in my head felt sad. Knowing no other way out, I accepted this new way of being me and covered up who I was and how I behaved in the world I lived in.

⌒

Speed through nine years, and I am in my kitchen with my mom and dad. We are discussing me going to see an R-rated movie with my friends. The movie was *Officer and a Gentleman*. Even back then I was a true believer in romance and love. I emphatically wanted to watch this movie, and they were concerned about the many mannerisms within it. Our discussion was based upon knowing the difference between sex with someone you love and sex with another person for pure physical enjoyment. Remember, I grew up in a stout Catholic family with all the doctrines that chastised us for disobeying the rule, the law, and the expectation of those older than us.

I recall sitting on the chair in a corner of the kitchen while they stood over me, thinking, "Do they even hear themselves?"

As they talked about topics like sex, drinking, and violence, my mind kept running with, "It is about love. Let me see it."

I realized we were on different paths. They were determined to have me be otherwise. As I listened to their arguments that day about not wanting me to condone the mannerisms I would bare witness to in the movie, I recall a heaviness in my chest. It was like a knowing that all they were saying was wrong in some way. Like any good child, I raised my right hand and promised to not pay attention to those mannerisms. And with that, I was allowed to see the movie.

To this day, it remains one of my favorite love stories of all time!

A few months later, I was told my parents were getting a divorce. Apparently, my father, the one who so eloquently spoke of sex as a by-product of love, had decided otherwise. Vividly, I remember the jolt to my heart as I entered back into the rated R conversation. He was lying. He was covering up. He was fake. And on that day, my trust in loved ones was shattered into a zillion pieces. The guilt took hold of my head and wrapped its ugliness in torments of the should'ves—you should have known he was lying, you should have seen he was lying, you should have felt he was lying. Trust became a small entity locked away in my Pandora's box. And from that moment on, I trusted little. My walls were stacked up, guarding my sensitive heart that pounded with fear if anyone came close. The new me was erected.

⌒

Inner beauty is a monologue we have within our Self. That monologue is constructed from various early occurrences that either allow us to see our Self and our beauty, or force us to live in a space of shame and confusion for what true beauty is. In our society, where beauty is an outward image and a construct pieced together with perfection, having an unbreakable definition of beauty is like air to functionality. It is nothing less than necessity.

My early experience did not teach me well that I had inner beauty. It taught me to negate my beauty and measure myself against the outward image known as beautification. The physical aspects of my body became a measurement tool for worth. This measuring was in direct denial of who I was. It became a constant for me to math it out—Is my hair like that person? Are my clothes good enough? Am I wearing the best makeup? Am I skinny enough? Is this the right way to eat? These simple yet devastating comparisons were crushing me to death. My inner script gave them so much power and strength that even when I would put the boxing gloves on and attempt to squash them, they revved up for a huge comeback.

love defined —
seeing and hearing are
tools for understanding

I lay there hearing the sounds of their intimacy. They were familiar sounds. I had talked about the meaning of those sounds before with them. I had seen them in the R-rated movie about love and sex. The interwoven sensual moans mixed with the feverish drive of a mission made sense. In one way, it was toe curling desperation, and in another it was hopeful joy. Hopeful took my heart away. My head explained what the sounds meant and my heart chimed in to agree this was love. The love they had talked about on so many occasions. The love I saw between them as they laughed and parented us. The love I knew existed. I closed my eyes and rested in peace and love.

—◁—

Upon arrival home from school in November of my Senior year of high school, we were asked to gather around the table. It seemed rather odd given our schedules. It was the middle of the afternoon, and this demand was unlike anything ever asked of us. They seemed adamant about their cause. I felt dizzy with a nervousness blanketing over me. I stared at them. I read no words. Nothing was being said on the outside, although my insides were rummaging through this container. The one that held us all in this space.

As I sat down in the heavy kitchen chair, the air was thick and seemed dark and dreary like a cool night in the early springtime. There was no laughter. There was only awkward silence. We all took a quick glance at each other, and they began to speak.

"We have something to tell you," is how they started.

The news shattered my heart in a zillion pieces. The fog that brewed around my head like a bonnet was filled with confusion, anger, and utter devastation. The world I knew, the world I felt safe in, the world I loved was being taken away. It would no longer exist as I had known it to be. What we were, gone forever and never to return.

I stared at them in awe of their reverence for the unemotional. She looked stunned and defeated. He looked agitated. Brother sat there and Sister ran to her room. I stood up totally numb and lost in the framework of sounds they had uttered to us. The randomness of this event running through my head as if the end result warranted a faster time. I caught a quick look at both of them unbeknownst of what would come next.

He came closer and asked if we could talk outside. I hesitantly agreed.

He looked at me and point-blank stated, "I just can't do this anymore."

No response from me. What did he expect me, a 17-year-old girl, to say?

He kept pleading, "I just don't want this anymore."

I frantically searched for words, anything, emotion…nothing!

I slowly moved away, tears in my eyes as he went to grab me. He wanted to hug me. I pushed away and shook my head as the tears began to ripple down my cheeks. My heart was searching reverently for the meaning of his words, for some sort of understanding that would justify his words, and for the love from a father to a daughter in her heartbreaking time of complete breakdown. I came up empty. Empty was how I felt in that moment. He took it all in one swoop of a phrase, "I just don't want this anymore."

Cloudy vision made the escape all the more difficult. Words, ideas, phrases were all whirling in my head like a tornado. All my heart had to say was, "You don't get to shatter my world and demand a hug." As I crept away in the slowest of all motions, I caught a glare at him...

Strangled in my confusion and devastation as a daughter who has heard her father say the unexplainable and the inexcusable, I crept up the stairs to my room.

As I slammed the bedroom door, all I could think about was, "Why me?"

Tears began to uncontrollably drain down my face. The pit of my stomach began to rumble as if a fistfight was brewing between what was and what is now. I laid there remembering and remembering and remembering.

We were not that connected. We did not really have talks to bring us closer. We did not even like the same things. He was the outdoor type—hunting, fishing, wearing Pendleton shirts. I was more reading books, hanging with my friends, and having fun listening to music. Our worlds clashed, and now our beings were clashing too. In that moment, I hated his words, I hated his simplicity for throwing it all away, I hated his timing of the day before Thanksgiving, and I hated him for choosing me.

As I lay there in my bed in the girly bedroom of a 17-year-old, I slowly melted away into the unknown. All I had been, who I was, gone forever. I was now defined by fear, anger, worry, and isolation.

Shame and guilt became my accessories. I shut my eyes and escaped for the night.

The next morning as I exited that bedroom and that night of unrest, I pulled up the mask that would now resonate as the "me" from this point on. I got clear about the role I was now expected to play. I had to take care of them. I had to be tough and wise and all-knowing and strong and brave and filled with courage beyond the norm.

A quiet voice within the depth of my Self questioned this move, but this new Self screamed loud and clear, "This is who we will be. This is how we will survive. Hurt will never be able to get to us again. Play the role and keep the mask on. No one will know."

going and gone—
following in his footsteps
left me lacking

Dad left the day before Thanksgiving, and in many ways never came back. He lived his truth coming and going as he wished. He lived in town for a brief period campaigning his truth. In the traditional sense of the family structure, it was difficult to fathom a father walking out on a child. Fathers are human and we, as society, often forget that aspect when assigning role descriptions.

The truth of our consciousness can paint a picture using absolutely no color. The imagination is a friend of the ego, and the ego must make sense of our pain using reversal illusion. It takes what is happening and reverses the story being felt into an imaginative tale to be understood by the masses.

For the days, months, years, and a handful of decades, this was the dialect being accounted for between him and me, the child. He told his tale, which would gather the masses to feel sorry for him and stand on his sideline in comfort for his pain. And I lived in silence. I once heard, "Silence is the most powerful scream."

From that moment on, I lived my new sense of Self silently covered in my mask. I played my role as a tough one letting no one see within my walls the utter chaos and sheer devastation of knowing one is not loved unconditionally. That unloving taught me well, and in the mirror of my life I saw unworthiness and unrecognizable shame for not being good enough.

Our lives mirror that which we feel on the insides of our bodies, deep down in our core. I suspect for my dad, he lived as an unloved human, and saw it as no grand gesture to give us breath yet take away our life that day. He was mirroring exactly what he bared witness to in his lifetime.

In the early years, I hated the man he could not be and the one he was. It was no saintly acquisition to quietly find peace within this experience. Today, I hold no blame toward him for leaving. He had to leave us, and in some way, he did gift us with life once again by leaving.

Yet the aftermath of that Thanksgiving eve is such a monumental expedition that I have carried for so many years in my core. The construct that evolved was a sense of lack. My lack of Self was so strong, it wiped out any knowing of love and belonging.

Completely unrecognizable to even myself, I began to hold those feelings within my body. We have energy centers that create lasting impressions as emotions flow through us. These free-flowing bits of energy can either expel or retract. If we allow our thoughts to move through us, there is high probability they will exit and never return. If our feelings are shame-influenced and guilt-ridden, they will stay around and take up residence within our cells and body systems, causing all kinds of tortured experiences.

Gut issues have plagued me for many years. Our middle section holds emotional energy from shame, unworthiness, anger, and self-acceptance. Abandonment issues can be felt in our hearts and our middle section. Because I shut down in silence and was unable to speak about my lack of trust, my Self-loathing, and my fear caused by such abandonment, I developed health challenges.

Habitual patterns of unworthiness continued. Although I didn't leave my children, I left myself many years ago. I operated behind my silence. Silence is golden, right? Well, not in this respect. Silence impoverished me into a tightly shut shelter for so many years. It imprisoned me to live as others saw me, and deep inside my core to live as one who is lacking and unworthy. Feeling unworthy and not good enough is a death grip on our soul. It functions as the Grim Reaper of your life in which the force of its existence allures you into a panic state of unpleasantness. The deadly state of such intense unworthiness robs you of a full and joyous life.

reckless revelations —
identity is built upon
experiences that leave
a lasting imprint

Growing up Catholic and eventually joining the Episcopal church, attending Sunday Mass was ingrained in the weekly ritual for living well. Attending Catholic school for eight years created a sound sense of the parable of the Prodigal Son. I had always had a love affair with that story and the ceremony of sacredness I felt within the service itself.

When I was little, I would pretend to deliver the body of Christ. Seriously, didn't everyone do that? I mean we would use Pringles broken into pieces and go up to each other and say, "Body of Christ." And the other would say, "Amen," and smile while they chewed the Pringle chip. Those words were blessings to my ears and my heart. I loved everything about that church ritual.

And then I did not. I left the church. Not so much physically, because I continued to attend Mass. In college, I attended a non-denominational service. The Word shared through verses, stories, and responses had meaning to me. It seemed to bring life to many of the dark corners of my every day and a calm to my nonexistence. It pumped me full of fuel, and on Sundays it was my fuel, much like taking your vehicle to the gas station and filling it up.

The story of the Prodigal Son was one that captured my attention. It is a story in which the beloved son of a wealthy father asks for some inheritance from his father. He leaves for what he thinks will be a better life. To his understanding and worldly views, life is harder than he ever thought and his choices are not always grounded in truth. When he lands himself at a crossroads, he decides to return home.

As he arrives home, his father welcomes him with open and loving arms. The father wishes to celebrate, and the older son who stayed and worked hard on the family property for years becomes angry.

The father looks at the oldest and responds, "My son, you are always with me and everything I have is yours. But we had to celebrate and be glad, because this brother of yours was dead and is alive again; he was lost and is found." (Luke 15:11-32 NIV)

My truest Self had been gone for many years, distracted by an unconsciousness that forced its perceptions upon my understanding and my being. These beliefs shadowed me within my own light.

I went for years thinking my love affair with Luke's verse was about co-workers, family, friends, neighbors, boyfriends, etc. Much to my denial, I thought it was about others. The lost one told the tale of everyone else and how they came into their own shining light. We can always see truth, honesty, and love in another and struggle walking that tightrope to view those very admirable traits within the depths of our own Self.

Back in 2014, I realized through God's synchronistic nourishment that it spoke to me. I was the lost son who had gone astray for reasons unknown to anyone. Something was calling me back. That something was a deep voice inside of my soul and my heart, barely audible yet loudly heard. I went through a few weeks when I kept seeing and hearing the story of the Prodigal Son. I was at a concert, and the musician told a version of the story to the audience. I was at a nondenominational bible study, and the story sprouted into the conversation. My two younger children came home from youth group and shared the story with me as it had slithered into their youth experience that night. God knows how to get our attention. Was I listening?

The word prodigal, a Latin derivative, means to *drive forth*. The story and this definition sent shivers through me like lightning on a stormy night. It was meant to be a calling back to myself. My thoughts had been reckless for so many years. The impressions created were not magically owned. They were remnants of garbage. I had spent my early life engaged in mindful warfare and battles between my heart and my ego. This story and my experiences were meant to drive me forward in to a grander knowing. A knowing that represented the ultimate love, and a love like no other. God will always welcome us home to our most authentic Self.

⌁

For a long time, I held tightly to my knowing that these impressions and these beliefs made me broken. Yet, at the same time, I would hear an ever-quiet breath lovingly speak to me, "You are special."

India.Arie says, "Your shadows make you whole!"

It has taken half a life to understand that the moments of impression that were deeply implanted in my heart could be repurposed for growth, for a clearer identity, and for a much-appreciated shadow-self of who I once was.

There is no need for shame or blame for these impressions that set the course of my earlier world. These experiences are enmeshed into an intricate pattern of development called learning.

We are impoverished by our stories filled with blame, shame, guilt, and unworthiness. It has never been about where our stories came from, but rather how our stories have shaped who we are NOT in this lifetime. Many of our stories have kept us from knowing ourselves, loving ourselves, and honoring all the gifts that God has bestowed upon us.

It can be somewhat of a mystery if we keep ourselves busy enough to continue the distraction. For me, this journey catapulted me to fall deep into the dungeon of asking, "Who am I?" and climbing my way out of that dungeon to a knowing of the answer to that all-time question.

A Course in Miracles calls this journey our curriculum. This makes so much sense to me. Sitting in the mirror of my own Self and the experiences I encountered has taught me many valuable insights and offered much wisdom. Allowing these moments and escapades to be learning opportunities was definitely a choice.

It seemed as though I was searching for something outside of the daily grind. Nothing ever really satisfied the hunger I had for peace and joy. As I delved into the pages of my so-called curriculum of learning, knowledge would enlighten me and yet still miss the mark of true understanding. A war would erupt in my heart that what I was deciding upon was being fought at all costs.

Our consciousness derives a story and conclusions based upon our illusive perception. The war between "who am I" and "who am I not" seemed to be a constant thread undermining each attack. This level of consciousness fighting me was not a known or comfortable place to be hanging out. It felt foreign and cold, while also loving and kind. Like a spark of fire just as it is beginning to burn, the questions began to ferociously take over my every thought.

My weakened state chose the easiest and most simplistic foundation as a way of explaining each experience.

"It must be me. Something is wrong with me. I am not worthy of goodness. I do not deserve good in my life. Good only happens to other people...never me."

Our identity is gleaned from snapshots of our experiences. Like a photo album, our identity is a construct pieced together from the puzzle pieces of the snapshots we have put onto each page of our life.

For each of my stories, my consciousness—or rather unconsciousness—lit up different aspects of Self in a selective process that allowed me to thread them into one mindful system.

This selectivity would graciously absorb the life force of my ego. Ego was ruthless in fighting its battles. These exploitations of my heart seemed to swirl around my mind long enough to join forces and construct my identity crisis. The falsehood within each belief was a sobering truth.

My mom asking me to not wear a halter to Vacation Bible School was not a shaming of MY body. It was a projection of her insecurities with body concepts handed to me behind the mask of motherly love. Was my mother loving? Absolutely!! Without a doubt!

One can only know that her admission of what to wear and not wear had more to do with her Self constructs than it was an admission of my lack of the perfect body. And my lack of consciousness, the ego, deceived me by borrowing her doubt and insecurity as a means for defining who I am.

My limited understanding facilitated the fear and the masks I wore for years. I was an Academy Award winner for playing the role of content, happy, and confident young one. Shielding my Self from a pain too monstrous to comprehend and a shattering that broke me into so many tiny crystalized formations. I became that tiny, broken, and hardened fighter. Contemplation quickly turned to weaponry designed to fight off the suffering I had become accustomed to having as a partner.

The ego shamed me into believing my unworthiness was cause for delayed living. My dad leaving the family was not a hatred of me; it was a self-hatred of himself projected onto me. The rubble of fear enveloped our family, and thus became our North Star for habitation.

My own awakening occurred in a moment when I realized the affair with the prodigal was just that—my own awakening. The mold needed to be re-framed. If you know anything about plaster, it is not Play-Doh. It does not easily take on a new shape just by force of pushing, pulling, and twisting. A beginning can only be obtained from a melting away of all that no longer looks good and a desire for something better, much better.

$$\sim$$

Our curriculum is not destined. We have a proverbial gold mine of free will. Free will is within our abundant reach.

A new course was being directed for me. A search and rescue operation to uncover the aspect of my truest, perfectly-born existence. The holiness within each of my misperceived stories was a chance for grace. God was inviting me to divine assistance as a means for coming home. This grace, held consciously in my heart, would guide me home to the me I had forgotten along the way.

I had become separated from an understanding of who I was. The impressions rebelled against this understanding and all-knowing. The once loving existence that I was at birth seemed to have gone astray and had forgotten that memory, the recollection, and the characters within that memory.

I needed to awaken. I knew it. I felt it. It was coming to swoop me off my feet as the most lucid love affair ever written in the stars.

Something whispered, "It will not be easy."

And my heart shouted, "Do it anyway. It will be worth it. You are worth it!"

And so I did.

I became the ultimate learner. I trashed the brick and mortar foundation that had constructed itself around me. I opened the door to a change and a growth. I begged and pleaded for me.

"Who am I?" I asked.

My heart spoke quietly and fiercely, "I am not sure."

Demolition of the misperceptions and misinterpreted stories had been scheduled. I knew the journey to my truth was already hidden in the upcoming dark storms. I would find a space with each of those storms, a dwelling so beautiful and peaceful. Each dwelling intended to be a joy-filled mansion of light and love.

I was on my way to the dwelling. The place of peace and love.

The place of me.

Me.

Phase 2: the DWELLING

*"Before I can tell my life what I want to do with it,
I must listen to my life telling me who I am. I must
listen for the truths and values at the heart of my
own identity, not the standards by which I must
live—but the standards by which I cannot help but
live if I am living my own life."*

-Herbert Alphonso

I lived in this space. Within the walls of my daily living, my inner thoughts and beliefs guided me, and my life taught me. I guarded this dwelling with a fierceness and a loyalty. The armor was in place to protect and shield from the pain I remembered and knew all too well.

Our experiences are lessons for learning. They are our curriculum. We must pay attention to the details and be our own learners.

Learning requires an expansion of some aspect within us, whether it be a thought process, a skill set, or a knowledge base. This expansion occurs as an organic evolution of change from what was to what is and even what can be.

‒⬡‒

We live our daily lives within the walls of our experiences. These opportunities afford us lessons to learn, to grow, and to thrive. Hillsong United sings a song entitled "Touch the Sky", which includes the phrase *"upward falling"*. Recognizing we cannot live this life by ourselves is a maturity gained by those who embrace a power larger than life. Humbly noticing your events and circumstances as open classrooms and you, therefore, as the student within the learning environment.

We build constructs around these occurrences as if we are building houses. These thoughts and beliefs derive from a foundational understanding of our Self. How we interpret this consciousness depends on our willingness to learn the lessons. The more willingness, the more learning; the more learning, the more consciousness; and the more consciousness, the more awareness that we are playing roles. Who we are within each occurrence remains the same. The role we play determines the cause of that occurrence, and our response to the cause ultimately identifies its effect as who we are.

losing —
amidst the rubble,
beauty arises

They said YES to the party, and we were elated. The deal was made. We were to help get the house cleaned up, the yard mowed, and the pool ready for the fun night with friends. She and I were ecstatic. The first item up was the mower to mow the lawn. I had never been on a riding lawn mower before. She said she had, although later I doubted if that was true.

She got on the lawn mower and turned the starter. I recall asking her through a nervous grin, "Do you know what you are doing?"

She laughed that belly laugh filled with nervous energy. I had heard that laugh before. It's the one that would result in us landing in the most serendipitously corrupt moment.

Her foot pushed downward on the gas, and the mower went breezing past me toward the door and the bush. In a flash, the mower was sitting on top of the bush as our eyes met. A fluttering laugh engulfed our air space, and we both went flying after the bush remnants in the mower cavity.

The remnants were then hidden far deep under trash in the bin. Anxiously, we breathed a sigh of relief. A close call we mindfully thought we had escaped until we heard him scream her name. In that moment of his treacherous piercing call to us, we knew he had found the half-eaten bush from the mower and the remnants in the trash bin.

For years, we would laugh uncontrollably about that moment on the mower.

‒◦‒

It was time for her to go. Our Texas-style shopping trip had come to an end. The laughter needed to mellow, and our worlds needed to go back.

Sitting in traffic that only a good morning flight would offer, we began to gather that nervous consoling we did to calm each other's nerves.

Mom dropped us off with intense directives, "Get in line, and I'll meet you inside the waiting area."

We hurriedly moved to those words. Got her boarding pass—check. Went through security—check. In those days, your whole party could red carpet you to the gate. And we did. Me, her, Mom, and that big mama suitcase. We seemed to be moving in slow motion amidst the entire airport system of others trying to get to their gates as well. So, in a flash, I grabbed that suitcase that was bigger than me and hoisted it onto my head and trotted to her gate. She and Mom were laughing so hard behind me as I bobbled between folks like the silver ball on a foosball table. We might have all peed in our pants that day, and that laughter will forever be imprinted in our memory.

But, she made her flight home.

‒◦‒

She wanted babies. So, the day I found out I was pregnant, she was the second one I told. We shared in that pregnancy and in that delivery. Son was born, and she was in the midst of all the love that day.

Room 10.

That birthing room delivered on cue a package that would change all of us for the better. She loved that little guy like her own. His love for her exploded a sense of calm in her and a purposeful essence. The two of them were inseparable, until she got sick.

She lived with that debilitating disease her whole life. We learned to operate from a place of gratitude, healthy thinking, and positive hope. We knew what hard work was and embraced the long road ahead. We gave power to our mind to construct a healthy vision for her. She had gotten sick before and came home shortly thereafter. We perceived these bumps as hurdles to endure. We used to look at each other and say, "Everybody has something." It was a choice to see life worth living.

She held my secrets and my stories, and I held hers. We were heart sisters bound by a family bond and a choice to spend our stories together. Laughter was our medicine. Daring each other to jump the hurdle that presented in the moment. Finding ourselves in inexcusable and completely neurotic experiences that always ended up in a new world view. She was my lifeline to family, friendship, and love—all things heart-infused.

And. Then. That. Day.

One. I. Will. Never. Forget.

I pulled up to the house and noticed the familiarity of the cars in the driveway. My mind started wondering. I walked in the house and ran into their eyes.

Why was my husband home?

Why was my mom at our house?

Why did they ask me to sit down?

I emphatically yelled, "NO!" I knew. My heart knew.

I heard what they were going to say before they even sent me the words.

I knew.

She was gone.

And a part of me left that day too. In a thick and ever still fog, I was lost. No light shining. No movement. Life still and sad. Heartbroken like never before.

I couldn't breathe. No air flow, no beating, my heart stopped. Tears could fill an ocean from my sadness. I was lost. I kept thinking I was bleeding because it hurt so bad. I couldn't find any blood. The pain was intense. It blanketed me. It's like perpetual nausea and suffocation. Air couldn't reach out of my lungs; sadness had a death grip around me immobilizing any movement.

And I was nine months' pregnant with my second child.

One week after her death, I began to have contractions. I wanted this baby, and I did not want to do this special moment without her. I refused to pack my bag. I took my toddler to a friend's house and drove myself to the hospital. I was numb. I was afraid. The false alarm was not funny and it sure did make me get ready. I knew it was her guiding me to bring this precious gift into the world. I fought her silently. Her excitement from the clouds and my numbness from the earth were not a match for heaven on earth. Love was hard work. Missing her sharing in my blessed moment was even harder.

One week later, I was drawn into the hospital yet again. This time, no false alarm. The real deal was here. It was time. As I entered the hospital, I was given a wheelchair. The nurse drove me to the birthing room in which I would deliver child number two. As we entered the room, I caught a glimpse at the room number.

Room 10.

She was there. She planned this moment to be amidst the love of this number two delivery in our family.

Guilt ran through my veins for weeks and months and years following her death. It was a long road of bad choices and rough conversations. Anger was my emotion of choice. I was mad she left. I was mad she was not here to share in the moments with me. When she was here, we enjoyed our present moments and belly giggled our way through anything.

I was not laughing now.

A couple years after her death, we were in my mom's kitchen with my love bugs, my children. They were two and four. The four-year-old happily announced, "Karen is here."

Our heads shot in his direction like a race car on a racetrack.

I bent down and said, "Sweetie, who is here?"

And he happily said it again, "Karen."

Stunned and quiet, I walked him over to her picture and said, "Honey, this is Aunt Karen."

He turned and galloped away and yelled, "Yep!"

It was a bolt of fresh air in my heart like skipping to your favorite song as a kid. I woke up that day to a knowing so complete and perfect. She was still with me.

And I smiled sweetly and knowingly.

⌒

I leaped that day. Not because I was no longer sad, but because of my sadness. The strong connection we had, and the sweet love we shared, was still available to me. I just needed to open my eyes to a possibility that life does not end. Life continues in different form.

There were signs I just did not see and hear.

In the hospital, in Room 10, on the day of the delivery without her, a nurse told me about a book to read. The book was Eckhart Tolle's *Power of Now*. That book was all about the present moment. That was Karen's subtle hint to keep my heart and mind in the present moment, and I would find her there.

Seeking to make sense of a painful event, like death and divorce, delays inner peace and evolution. According to Dr. Caroline Leaf in her book, *Switch on Your Brain*, it can literally stunt your growth. The neo-cortex is the part of the brain that is charged with logic and sequential reasoning. The limbic system is solely about decision-making and behavior driven from emotions and feelings. These two do not play well together. They are actually a contrast of nuances. Both are in the boxing ring fighting for an understanding.

One part of us is actively seeking reasoning for why such tragedy occurs. The other part of our brain is filled with such emotional devastation that contradicts any logical formation. The violent churning of these nuances blocks the possibility for acceptance in any form of such events. And without acceptance of such an event, the change involved in growth lends itself nonexistent.

We sacrifice our natural tendency to grow and move forward from pain for the logical tightrope of fear. We are so wired for connection that if we logically make sense of not connecting, it frames a cold-hearted entity. Thus, we plant our Self in a garden of a never-ending torture chamber neither growing nor connecting. The spiral of fear keeps us entangled in a constant dialect of perpetual anger, doubt, resentment, guilt, and silence.

Freedom is only found in the present moment. In the tiny snippet lies a possibility, and an invitation to awaken from the darkest hour to a light guided by our soul's desire to breathe. This ever-so-small moment in time can be the spark that enlightens us to a changed reality. There can be beauty after death collapses a life and a love.

⌒

I painted myself back to life. Each day finding the colors to work with, trying out new gadgets, and letting my heart speak. There was grave pain and agony. Excavating the dark corners of past regrets, painful fun, words unsaid, and stories unfinished. Finding the new vision from the same deeply affectionate love we shared. Painting a new picture with her not in it became beautiful works of love and wholeheartedness. From the rubble of a collapse, beauty can arise.

in the present—
only in the present moment
can we find and be who we are

About 12 or so years ago, I wanted another baby. I kept telling my husband, who was in finance and accounting and very logical, that, "I felt someone was missing."

We had extensive talks about the money, the work, the living space (we lived in a comfortable three-bedroom house). In every conversation we had, it made absolutely no logical sense whatsoever to have another child. Having kids is never logical—it's expensive, it's exhausting, it's stressful, and it's just plain nuts.

I couldn't shake the feeling, and my husband knew it. I even said to him at one point in the dialogue, "Listen, I get this makes no sense at all, and it's completely crazy. AND I can't shake the feeling that someone is missing when we all sit on the bed and watch movies. I feel like there is another person who is supposed to be here with us."

My husband finally agreed. And I got pregnant. I was sooo excited!!! I had two boys and everyone kept inquiring about wanting a girl. Of course, I gave the proper answer, "I just want a healthy baby."

It really was the truth. I believed wholeheartedly in the art of visualization, and the power of our thoughts and our words. I did not want to jinx karma and my good fortune with a desire for anything but a healthy young one.

I was 38 and apparently, when you are older and having a baby, you get all kinds of free gifts. One of the free gifts was an extra ultrasound to check on the healthy baby. I loved those little pics, so I said, "Yes!" We talked about the "what ifs."

What if there are problems or complications?

What if something happens?

We decided it didn't matter. Nothing mattered. We wanted a baby.

We scheduled the ultrasound for week 11, and I showed up by myself. My husband was not there. He had to be out of town, and we couldn't change the date of the ultrasound due to the developmental stage of the baby. So, I went by myself. I left work and told the ladies I worked with that I'd be back in a bit, like an hour or so. None of the other ultrasounds took very long. And I had no evidence this one would be any different. The other two ultrasounds were the same: The nurse technician would squeeze some jelly on your belly, and snap a few pics of legs, arms, butt, face, heart, etc. And you were done.

As I got called into the ultrasound room, if I am being honest, I was a bit nervous. It's that feeling of uncertainty that can completely put you in chains of fear at times. The nurse put the jelly on my stomach and began pushing buttons and rolling the wand over my belly. She didn't say anything and after a bit of time, I began to worry. I don't know about you, but when I get nervous, my hands get moist, my heart beats faster, and my mouth goes dry. I even think I started to shake a bit. I had a hard time breathing efficiently, especially given I was lying on my back.

It seemed as if everything about that moment was moving in very slow motion. And, of course, all the toxic thoughts and worries came flooding into my head—*There's no baby* was the big one that kept grabbing my attention.

I sat there as she turned off the machine and asked me to lie still. She quietly and calmly looked at me and began to talk, "Honey! I've got to tell you something."

(Oh my gosh! I was about to throw up!)

She continued, "You've got two babies in there."

My mouth fell open. I even think my heart stopped. Tears swelled in my eyes, and I gasped for air as I whimpered to her, "What?"

She sort of gave a chuckle and confirmed. I had to sit up. I couldn't breathe. She asked, "I guess this wasn't planned, huh?"

I wanted to shout, "Uh, NO!!!"

One freaking baby is all I wanted. One more in the mix on the bed watching movies. What the hell am I going to do with two...two babies AT. ONE. TIME?!?!?!

She took the amazing pics of those two babies, and I laid back to cry. I was completely freaked out. As I left, they were all so kind and loving (I think they were worried about me). At one point, I mentioned to the nurse, "Don't worry! I will like them." She got the biggest chuckle out of my guilty mother oath!

I pushed the button to get into the elevator. I got in and could not remember what floor to get off. I cried. The elevator opened, and I had no idea how to get to my car. I cried. I stayed in the elevator as a nurse with a gurney got on. I cried. Each time the elevator stopped, I cried. I had no idea how to get to my car.

I finally ended up at my car and, in that moment, I wanted my mom. You know that one person who can provide comfort...who listens…who hugs you and all the troubles melt away. I wanted THAT in that moment.

I was also smart enough to know, if I didn't tell my husband and instead went to my mom first, my problems on the home front were going to be BIG. Really big! Remember, he was out of town.

So, I decide to call him. He answered, "Hey, what's up?"

(You need to know that he was well aware I had the ultrasound and the time it was scheduled. So, his voice was clear with a touch of anxiety.)

The minute I heard his voice, I began to uncontrollably sob, like the kind with snot and ugly noises where you literally lose your voice to air and blubbery sounds. He was now a bit softer yet intense as he asked me, "Honey, what is wrong?"

I replied to his question with a blubbering and snot-induced whimper, "We have two babies in there." And with that last sound came the barreling of snorts, snot, and cries even louder than before. I could not close the floodgates of water pouring from my eye sockets.

After the prego pause, he said to me, "Oh, Honey. It will be alright. This just means we have to focus a little bit more on our family… on what matters."

That moment of finding out we were having twins and telling my husband as he was driving to the airport, forever changed my life. His exclamation of truth in the moment became our vision. Our family mantra was delivered in that moment of truth, honesty, and blubbering snot running down my nose. Family matters. Focus on what matters.

I cried for weeks anytime family, a friend, or a colleague would speak of twins. I lost my air along the way many times. It was a constant battle between my head versus my heart.

Two kids now. Two kids coming. Four kids forever.

Could I handle this?

How would I do this parenting thing?

Fear intermingled with love and excitement like socializing at a cocktail party. Slow and steady breathing flowed between the bumps of panic and utter unease.

My planning Self stayed busy researching all the basics, finding out what to do and how to do it. My heart remained laser focused on appreciating each person who helped us, each parent I met who offered advice, and each laugh I was able to muster up in anticipation of the love-filled chaos we were about to embark on.

―◠―

The present moment is all that matters. I really did not have a clear understanding for what that was until that moment when the nurse said those life-changing words, "You have two babies in there."

THAT out-of-body paradox brought me directly into the present moment. I became so still from her words that I could hear my heart thump to its own beat like a drum, could feel my breath move slowly in and out of my lungs like a balloon, and could see the movable parts within the room as if it was all in a slow-motion video. My present moment was birthed.

Eckhart Tolle describes this kind of interaction between thinking and feeling as *"noise-making."* Too often we quickly revert to thinking because we, humans, are not knowledgeable and comfortable with emotions.

He says, "*Emotion literally means 'disturbance.' The word comes from the Latin emovere, meaning "to disturb."*"

We don't like this disturbance within our bodies; therefore, we easily choose to grab hold of our thoughts. Our thoughts are comforting. We allow the logic of our deceiving mindfulness to convince our pain to play a bigger role than even needed. We lose trust in our ability to convey honestly what an event conjures up.

I had forgotten my own strength in that moment of attentiveness. I had forgotten that God provides living events and the support to live them well. I had forgotten who I was in that moment of truth about my upcoming family additions.

In my unforgotten state, I projected fear into a whirlwind tornado of negative thoughts, toxic emotions, and scathing beliefs.

⟶

Two years later, I found myself sitting on the stairs in my new house and crying uncontrollably. I was miserable: exhausted, numb, and completely drained. The guilt from such intensity blanketed me. My heart knew I had wanted to be a mother and knew, without a doubt, this role was my calling with all of its bells and whistles, and rusted intersections.

Who am I?

Why can't I do this?

Once again, curiosity flooded my daily calm. This parenting thing could not be that much different than schooling those youngsters in the classroom for 167 days of the year. Teaching and parenting had to be collateral beauty markers. I had been exposed to these habitual markings for many years during my teaching days. I know the sensation when facing all those minor faces filled with energy, excitement, and unlimited potential for adaptation. I remembered all too well that every year, for the decade of years I taught in the classroom, how I would roll into the holiday season with my mind mush like mashed potatoes served at the Thanksgiving meal, and my body heavily weighed down from too little sleep, too much adrenaline, and lack of self-exposure to peace.

In my tearful sense on the stairs that day, and along with an episode of Oprah that happened to be on the television playing in the background, I was catapulted in another change and a new direction.

A New Earth by Eckhart Tolle brought me out of the stink and into a brighter, shinier version of my reality. The interview between he and Oprah that day resonated with my inner mumble for help. *A New Earth* was presented as, "Encouraging its readers to live their lives in each present moment and create happiness for themselves." Tolle emphasized the book's purpose, "To not add new information or beliefs to the mind or try to convince the reader of anything, but to bring about a shift in consciousness."

He referred to "*the nightmare of the pain-body experience* as one in which we carried in our knapsacks stories that were never ours to carry along. We, at young ages, were meant to be only observers and no one ever told us that respect for ourselves. So, instead, we took on the stories and the painful energy truth of it in our bodies. These stories morphed into physiological abscesses leaking judgement, doubt, ridicule, embarrassment, guilt and a rash of self-loathing. A simple event turned into a torment of agony leaves us with an unconsciousness for life."

The twins were my alarm clock. They woke me to a deeper understanding for who I was and an appreciation for the lighter side of living well. They taught me what mattered and helped me surrender and release that which did not serve me well. They kept me hyper-vigilant on my ego state of mind. They brought me back to earth and gifted me a new outlook on who I was and who we were as a family.

My little teachers forced me to uncover my masks and the costumes I had been wearing for years. They dissected my old stories and aided in rewriting new versions of the old characters of victimization. The illusions I had created became flushed out with beloved synchronicity. The patterned signs and symbols magically appeared from behind the scene. God orchestrated these love bugs to thread together a love story with me, myself and I.

Thankfulness became a way of breathing through each moment. Blocking off the activity that tried desperately to govern my mind. Locating an appreciation for each building block that was gently and lovingly put in place to construct our timeline together. Willing to grasp the tiniest bit of heaven from each situation, each event, and each moment. Letting go of filth and toxicity. Keeping our world clean as a visionary with super eye strength. Holding on to God's hand in our everyday survival as the one and only force to never reckon with and trusting in his superpower tendencies.

Finding that present moment in the rubble of a collapse, gratifying it as the most sacred of all callings, charged me forward into who I was that had been lost.

changing locations —
the sacred space determines
what is found

The hope of every storm we encounter is a knowing that there will be a rainbow of gorgeous, fiery brightness afterward. And that year, we were in a storm.

The twins were two and running amok of our house and our energy sources. We were drained. Sometimes our best laid plans changed directions in an instant, and trusting in the power of God to know more sounds good to the ear and yet can be a challenging dilemma to the heart.

When the twins were born, we lived in a small three-bedroom home. We had planned to move when the twins were three, knowing we would be needing a much bigger house at that point as they moved from the crib to toddler beds. Once again, our best laid plans would quickly take a different detour.

Our Son was having some difficulties finding where he belonged within the school community he was attending. We fought the hard fight to understand both sides of the classroom learning experience. The battle we were having did not seem to have a favorable ending. All parties believed in their perceptive truths.

The light bulb went on one day when I watched him suffering in a way that no child at the age of seven should be feeling. As an educator and as a mom, it broke my heart to watch him on the couch, teary-eyed and nervously twirling his hair into tiny points while staring blindly at the television.

THIS. WAS. NOT. MY. BOY.

When we are faced with changing a situation, and we see no way out of it, the freedom we have as individuals guides us to make the self-caring decision to get out, let go, and surrender. And that is what we did. A year before we were ready, financially and emotionally, we let go of a plan and surrendered to God's knowing what was best. We moved our home and our family to escape a no-win situation.

We were scared and a bit out of sorts to find a place that would be our forever family residence. We wrestled with what we needed and what we wanted. When the realtor spoke, "See the possibility, not the reality," that was a sure sign we were finding our sacred space to encounter our new life together and our new lessons of learning.

The new dwelling felt good, and all aspects of what we needed and wanted seemed to align into this beautiful dwelling. We overlooked the minor flaws to see beyond the outward appearance. We watched the synchronicities of a space become our place to love together, to live together, and to grow together.

Little did we know these four walls, with all of its interior challenges, would become our grandest classroom to find what had once been lost. Those things that are most sacred can often make us scared because they are the inner workings of our heart.

—

God is my Superhero. He heroically shows up for me when protection is needed. He has always been my Guiding Light for goodness, for love, and for my highest Self to be present. He, along with the Angels, have ushered important guidance in my life. This Spiritual

Realm is a sacred sanctuary where I find complete safety, security, and unconditional love.

Prayer has never changed my outer scenario, even when I begged and pleaded. Believe me, I tried on many occasions to ward off outer circumstances with my eyes closed, fists clenched, and a stern insistence in prayer. Instead, it catapulted an explosion of inner dialogue to manifest. Prayer is a continual chain linked together with gratitude, surrendering, and stillness.

"Be still and know that I am God." Psalm 46:10

The answers never came in the busyness of distractions and running around. I could only hear him…his voice…his guidance…his plan…and my heartbeat when I got still.

Meditation became the answer to a prayer for a healthy way to respond to life. Healthy is an interesting word. If you peel it apart, it becomes *heal + thy*.

So, in the midst of some not-so-calm years, I desperately needed to be a healthy Self. In essence, the Universe was guiding me toward healing thy Self. We both had the same vision. It continually became obvious that God and the Universe always knew what I needed, even if I was a bit obstructed in my vision.

The moments of stillness became my fortitude. I found myself hiding in the shadows of my beliefs, ideals, and fundamentally my world. Meditation changes the structural makeup of who we are. It held answers for me and insights into aspects I had never considered.

Thich Nhat Hanh tells us, "Meditation can help us embrace our worries, our fear, our anger; and that is very HEALING. We let our own natural capacity of healing to do the work."

My human ego would manifest fearful predicaments within my head and offer no guidance to escape. It robbed me of all hope, and seemed to merge a new framework for conducting life. It played big, which rippled into more and more anger. It took many stumbles before the alarm went off awakening me to a much-needed new way of living.

A Course in Miracles says, "We are either loving or fearing."

My heart spoke in an ever-so-soft, shaky voice, "Sweetie, you are so scared of yourself. Open up and let me in."

This message spoke to me on so many occasions through situations, through people, and through language that would appear in my inbox. When we decide to heal our Self and return to love, God finds a way for us to come back home.

Meditation was, and still is, the vehicle for finding me, hearing me, and listening to what God had for me. The silence was not void; it had ALL the answers I needed.

⌒

Within the dwelling of my own heart, all my life was planned. My heart held the answers I needed when the ego raised questions, batted its disapproving finger, and seemed to regulate my joy.

I hated the ego for its fierceness. I despised its love for what I thought was the inevitable. It seemed to take advantage of my loyalty. And I was a good student. I listened well to its messaging, and even allowed it to brand who I was.

Know thyself. Heal thyself. Love thyself.

Awakening to an ever-expansive eye opening taught me the impact of the present moment, that beauty can be found, and sacred spaces are rich in learning. Opening my eyes in this way led to a detour that afforded me a heart opening unlike any other. Filled with love not because life was perfectly laid out, but in spite of its imperfections, love was at the core of the beating.

Letting these learnings teach me to trust my heart to beat again, to love deeper, and to give God all my appreciation in such miraculous ways.

Although the dwelling had fallen apart, it gave way to new beginnings and the totality of a renovation.

Phase 3:
the RENOVATION

So if I stand let me stand on the promise
That you will pull me through
And if I can't, let me fall on the grace
That first brought me to You
And if I sing let me sing for the joy
That has born in me these songs
And if I weep let it be as a man
Who is longing for his home
-Rich Mullins

Our life, filled with many present moments, is our grandest educator. And, when it teaches you to love, many changes must take place within your heart and your head. Knowing thyself is ultimately our greatest challenge and our greatest accomplishment. Tearing down the barriers to loving ourselves and rebuilding a structure sustainable with compassion and acceptance is hard work. It must be met with a single fortitude of governance. Gratitude. Patience. And a willingness to learn in all ways. These are the building blocks to a new structure and a new way of living life.

When we are confronted to change through a synchronicity of unexplainable events, it is our duty to our body, mind, and soul to listen and take note. This is our life teaching us that what once was, will no longer work. And this lesson of learning must ignite and inspire a power up to change our own Self—our inner dialogues, our inner existence, and our outer circumstances. Tearing down our beliefs, our thought patterns, and our habitual practices of toxic emotions is where the renovating begins. It is not possible to sustain fundamental changes on the same foundational system that failed to work. Knowing who we are is the goal. Aligning our daily life and our decision-making from an all-knowing within our loving heart is truth and the way.

The spirit that soars through our bloodstream renews itself by challenging the very structure that has been in place. Limitation is not seen as negative, but a mere door to open. Listening becomes a life force. Acting on it becomes the journey.

walking away —
hearing only occurs when
we let go and listen

The age of eight found me making worksheets and creating lessons for my pretend "students." Teaching was in my blood. It encompassed all of who I thought I was—the one who taught as well as the one who learned.

It was not a question would I, yet more of a, "*Where will I be planted and whom shall I serve?*"

I patiently waited for my own students, my own classroom, and all the interesting ways we could learn together. My students, the ones I would shape, inspire to grow, and help in all ways, would be my family and an extension of me. I would find myself dreaming of that space, the four walls decorated and filled with the invitation for their best. I researched the best way to teach them well. I excelled in all the classes that would make me the very best teacher. I knew this role well, and I was good at it.

One professor fed me exactly what I needed to hear to confirm my dream come true, saying, "You have a knack for taking what works in the research and implementing it into practical ways that will benefit your students."

I found myself in a school and a classroom, my classroom, teaching all aspects of life to my students. Parents entrusted me to instruct their individual one. I engaged their mind, body, and hearts as I ensured all aspects of learning made sense for each of them. I was complete in the realm of teaching and learning.

I knew my heart was in a resting place each time I taught, and that peace was a bounding force. It came as natural as a sunset on a cool spring evening. My mind was wired for this capacity to change minds, mold hearts, and enlighten our young ones. My fueled fondness for all things school was my lifeline for years.

"What do you do?" they would ask.

"I am a teacher," I would confidently reply, without any hesitation.

It ran through my veins like blood. I ate it up, thought about it all the time, dug deep for "THE BEST" way to help them learn. I read every book, and attended as many workshops as I could. It was the lens for how I saw life and the world I lived in.

The young ones were my first love as a teacher, followed by the adult learners becoming my niche within the boundaries of the teaching and learning world. Educational enthusiasm for all aspects of learning sparked such light and vibrancy in me. Once called a walking encyclopedia for education, I understood the broader capacity for growth and development.

The voice began in short snippets of quiet moments in deep thought. I knew what was being asked of me and shook my head in disbelief. It had to be wrong. How could I be asked such a thing?

I didn't want to leave, yet the force pulling me away became obvious on a daily basis. The suffocation of my fire struck a chord and my music was definitely out of tune. In fact, there were days my music was nonexistent.

That road trip consumed my life and my energy for almost two years, until, in a split second of desperation, I got it. In a state of love-filled panic, I gave my notice. It felt like a bad dream. Something deep within me knew my light was dimming, and I was crumbling amidst the foundation I thought was me. Education, schools, classrooms, learning, and mentoring adults to teach better were my life force for so many years, and I was walking away.

In May 2015, within the last few weeks of the school year, I rode the roller coaster between high moments of elation celebrating all I had believed in, knew well, and taught others in the course of my education career, and the lows of losing a part of my skin, my breath, and my identity.

The last day came with a vengeance—a celebratory ongoing and a quiet retreat. Floods of tears ran from my eyes as I drove away from what was my life and the source of air I breathed for so long.

The quiet moments before the move, and the ones following, were speaking wisdom into my ears. My heart listened with anticipation for newness, and at the same time, bore the sadness of a world unknown.

The quest for what I would do next following my departure became the everyday action-packed drama. This mission of search and rescue for who I was ignited a bright awakening I had not known before.

My days filled with quiet moments of solitude and listening— hearing the voice tell me to trust a plan bigger than myself, hearing my heart pleased with my awakening, hearing dreams I had not known existed begin to breathe again.

Letting go of the identity of who I was…a teacher…one who educates…gave me the freedom to see, to hear, and to know…I am a teacher, still.

My platform would change, my mantras shifted, and learning in a much bigger and broader spectrum began to evolve from the lost dwelling place within me. I found a joy unknown to me in my previous classroom and very much alive as a lost part of me.

─○─

In the book, *The Good and Beautiful God: Falling in Love with the God Jesus Knows* by James Bryan Smith, Smith discusses the three primary influences on, *"Who we are and how we interpret our life."* He explains these influences as, *"Our narratives (how we think about God), our spiritual disciplines (how we practice being God-like), and our social contexts (whom we interact with)."* Smith goes on to demonstrate how these influences shape the mind, the body, and the social context of who we are. Our bodies are receptors for knowing. They can determine what is best for us. Through the senses, the body receives signals. These bodily signals communicate to the mind, which in turn articulates the messaging to our will. Our will decides how we participate in our life socially.

I would find myself in such elation each time I encountered a context for teaching and learning. My body linked those good feelings to my mind and eventually my will, letting me know I was in my element. I first became aware of those good feelings when my younger me pretended to teach students with my handmade worksheets and my pretend classroom for learning. As I grew into my own learning institution, I recognized those all-powerful feelings and attached my identity as a confirmation of who I was. My limited experience defined teaching and learning within the walls of a school classroom. I think God knew teaching and learning included a much bigger and broader arena.

Our bodies work as traffic lights for each of us. When they sense we, as humans, are not traveling in the right direction, they signal for us how to proceed forward. It is our role to listen with our head and our heart, and hear the directive.

The quick and easy disruptions in our human society can bring us down the wrong lens of understanding on our journey. We confuse "*This is not working for you anymore. Time to move on.*" with, "*You are not working hard. Work harder.*" We mistake the signals of stress induced as a message to do more. We misread the signs and often get scared. The voice deep within us knows we are being signaled for sacred work. Yet, our egoic fear takes over and we frantically search for comfort. This interpretation misleads us in believing we are wrong, unworthy, and not good enough. We settle for the comfort and work harder, often in the wrong direction.

We let the outer experience shame us into believing in our limitations and our unworthiness. Thus, the changes we make are not for the better, but rather they are changes reinforcing more fear within us. This fear becomes the governing force holding us hostage in the same old daily life habits and patterns.

Smith writes in his book, "We cannot simply change by saying, I want to change. We have to examine what we think (our narratives), how we live daily (our spiritual discipline) and who we are interacting with (our social context)."

When we let go of our will and our past narrative, we allow God to gift us his vision for our purpose. What we let go of will never be lost, but becomes a thing of collateral beauty.

I am a teacher. This me was not lost when I walked away from the school system. In letting it go for the short term, it was allowed to reawaken within me and include a larger-than-life spectrum for gaining inner wisdom from my own Self and my own life experiences. My context for learning grew to a deeper understanding.

Although the context has changed, the message and the discipline remained intact. Renovating the inner dialogue and my whole understanding of who I was, allowed me to infuse fresh and unlimited perspective into the solid foundation of knowing who I am.

the clearing —
shedding the old makes
way for the new

The boxes and the dust consumed my space. The things I once found precious did not seem to hold the same meaning as before. For hours, I would sit and stare blankly at these items.

What did this item mean to me? The chains around my neck got tighter.

Who gave it to me? My chest tightened up.

What do I want to do? My mind raced here and there.

What am I to do? Nothing.

Who am I? Tears, silence, and a tightened nothing.

I wanted to breathe. I wanted to smile again. I wanted to hear what my heart already knew.

I started in my dresser, partly because it was easier to stomach. Each item held a story, a past, an experience, and a piece of my heart. From room to room, I cleaned out drawers, closets, boxes, and shelves. The entire house had been scraped and prodded. The past was losing its fight to stay in the pole position. The tears I gathered while disposing of these items could fill a swimming pool. I had created an attachment to the stories.

They told who I was.

Or so I thought.

The more bags I filled, the lighter I felt. The more boxes I gave away, the clearer I was thinking. The more items I gave away, breathing became smoother.

Amidst the rubble of years and years of me, I felt commissioned to build again. Tearing down the walls of past experiences brought me an awareness that many good and joyful moments were had by all involved and the joy felt in my heart was worth more than the objects sitting on the shelf in a dusty closet.

Blessing those who intended to send me love, and offering forward the gifts to serve another, seemed to bring about a new-found intellect. Accepting the books and the paperwork as having already accomplished the goal, and wishing them onward to seduce another, brought me a sense of calm and peace I had not felt before.

Carrying the items up and out of the tightly packed shelves, drawers, closets, and boxes enforced a wild excitement and built me up to warrior status.

Months and months of rearranging took its toll on me. Feeling energized and withdrawn can lead to a confusion of sorts.

The boxes and bags and items were gone. All given away to a new life for another human. And I felt left with a barren existence like being naked in a public forum.

Who was I?

I had invested my lifetime in thinking one way and believing in that identity and vision. The voice I heard in the quiet stillness supported the clearing and jumped for joy at the freedom that appeared within the walls of my life. Yet, I was more distraught with no answer to my ever-growing need for an answer.

～

Our narratives need to be cleaned out and changed to accommodate a healthier way of living.

A quote by Malcolm Muggeridge from his own journey in life seemed to alert a sense of energy within the dullness I was feeling. He says, "We need to find God, and He cannot be found in noise and restlessness. God is the friend of silence. We need silence to be able to touch souls. The essential thing is not what we say, but what God says to us and through us."

I began to understand. My life had been filled with so much clutter, I could not make sense of what was working and what was not working; what was good for me and what was not healthy for me; who was helping me grow and who was holding me back. Claustrophobia occurred as circumstances shoved me into the tight, dark crevices of my life. Too many things and people cluttered my mind and my inner dialogue, causing me to be distracted. The strangling of misread moments in waves causing sudden shifts of everyday living. Expectations from the outer world bombarded my thinking and drove me into traffic jams of chaos.

This clutter extravaganza needed to be broken apart. Experience by experience, person by person, and item by item had to be examined for its benefit to a healthier version of living freely and truthfully. A silence had to be found.

Breathing has power that far exceeds our earthly maneuvers. Catching my breath gave me all that had become lost in the shuffle of growing up, family dynamics, and the constant changes life offered.

Stopping and slowing down allowed me to hear what was being articulated to me about who I was and what I was meant to be.

Our bodies signal when a stop is needed. A shutdown of all that once had meaning in order to discern the true significance. Assessing whether we have a connection to God-like living and God-like being forces us to forego what was for an unlimited potential of possibilities.

Getting still and quiet was not easy. In the beginning, the breath wanted the fast pace urgency. Boxing gloves literally worked each breath into slow motion. Inner conversation was met with a loving, "Not now. Only quiet is allowed."

A quote appeared in my inbox one day that gave me strength to continue to expand the quiet, in my mind and in my life. Sadie Nardini, a yoga teacher and spiritual teacher, said, "Letting the tough stuff emerge is the starting point for realigning with who you are."

My tough stuff—the beliefs blocked by the shadows of people, the residue of experiences, and the impurity of my own understanding—had to emerge. And the only way for it to rise up was for me to unload all the distractions and all the objects weighing me down. It was a tough and bold move, and one that saved my life.

Getting rid of all that was not working for me and that which did not bring me joy connected me to an inner source of power. This power within us always exists. It was always there within me. Tuning into it can be tricky for those of us who dance with the life force outside of us. I had been dancing to the outer music of my life for years. Paying attention to the fullness of my breathing and placing my body in utter stillness gave me air to fight the attack of my outer narratives. It proved to be the exact medicine to awaken me from a slumber, like the gentle kiss in *Sleeping Beauty*.

the attack—
the sudden impact
of an attack is only
a detour to keep on
our own loving path

I sat reading. Uncontrollably shaking. Spit welling up in my mouth and the violent pulse of a gut about to embark on an up-and-out explosion. Eyes blinded with the liquid of confusion and terror. The words cut deep; the message deeper. My heart broke open while the blood slowly drizzled out. I grabbed at the air around me desperately wanting to catch it so I could breathe. It kept slipping through my hands.

The pain was real. Her words were all too familiar. I had felt this before. I had been in this exact spot before.

This was conditional love.

Do what I want and I will show you affection.

Do what I need and I will show you love.

Do what I can handle and I will accept you.

Do what I know and I will let you stay.

BUT… This time was different. Even in the same feeling of a memorable pain, something was different.

I knew all too well how this version ended before. I was lost and unrecognizable. I was quiet and the voice was buried. This time was different. Something was different.

Her words in an email sent at the end of a night, "I was hurt and sad that you had such feelings of disgust for me upon our first interaction."

I sat there in stunned isolation. My words, a week before, said to her at a book study on judgement and love: "When I first met you, you drove me crazy. All the talking you would do at the events we were at. I realized I didn't know you and once I got to know you, I shifted my perception. Now I do not feel that way anymore. I see you as loving and kind."

In the moment the words came out, I could feel her eyes smack me down. Her words followed, "You're one to talk."

I tried to explain, and she shut it off. Closed her ears and her heart to hearing what I was saying, what I was meaning, and how my words and my story were an admittance of MY wrong judgment. She made it about her. It was not about her. It was about MY learning.

Six days later, she shared her hurt, fighting back with her words.

We were one. In a group, together representing a collective of love, compassion, unity, and faith. For months we sat together, shared our deepest inner Self, our struggles, our fears, and our successes. Our stories were all the same...pain, trauma, not being seen or heard for who we really are at the core of our being. Fighting our inner battles with our only known and understood weapons—the surrender of our human shell for a wholehearted Self.

I crumbled upon her words—she kicked me out of the circle evidenced with me not being safe, me not being trustworthy, me not being vulnerable, and me not being honest. Forever shunned because I shared too much of the truth, my truth, my honesty, my raw and real tribulation of learning, and a coming home to a new me… more loving, more awakened to what matters, and less inviting of the extravagant show on display. I removed my barriers to love and invited in the real learning to wipe me clean and help me shine.

This sense of humor from the Universe felt familiar. I knew I had been in the exact same space and feeling the exact sameness as before. And…yet, this time was different. Something was different.

Embarrassment glided over me. Sorrow for missing out crept within me. Hurt sucker punched me in the gut. The pain was real. The hurt was real.

And I was real within the pain and the hurt. Something was different.

For the first time, I heard the voice, my soul speaking up, from deep within the depths of my inner hidden world whimper, "You will survive this. You are stronger than you think."

And I knew, in that moment of extreme pain, that my Self was untouched. I felt the warmth of its hug and nurture. I heard the loving kisses it blew my way to wipe away the physical tears that were ascending downward across my face. The real me, my soul, my true Self, was rising freely within this fireball of attack from another. This time was different. The ego did not win with its illusions and toxic thought processes. Instead, the soul emerged in love to care for my Self and wrap my Self in a coat of armor decorated with only goodness, worthiness, being enough, and pure love.

‑‑◯‑‑

The great mystery within a conscious life is that out of bad, toxic, and negative experiences, we, the human being, can rise into a more awakened awareness. This awareness brings with it divine charisma, a freedom to love ourselves as we are, and an all-powerful knowing that we, the human being, are nothing less than perfect love. Growth is a spiral staircase to be climbed one step at a time and curving around to absorb the continual happenings in order for us to gain a mastery in learning to love. Our Self has to walk that spiral staircase so that we learn our individualized lessons along the way toward upward movement.

This experience is handed to us on a silver platter as a mechanism for our revelation that we are worthy, whole, and love with God. He is our connector to life, the brightest of lights, and a true consciousness. Our dynamic process for awakening to God's presence is a call to action.

Our evolution requires moments of joy and moments of attack. It is within the duality of these polar opposites that a pulse and a fire exist. Igniting that pulse and becoming a fire starter is the beginning of the journey to come home.

Once the awakening begins, there is no going back in time. Escaping into the dark crevices cannot occur. Toxic thinking seems silly and illusive. The realness of the knowing that we, the human being, are consciously called to the duality of living captured in the retreat of love and light.

⌒

Renovation is a call to action. It is the change agent inviting us to learn deeper, believe stronger, and know without a doubt.

Attacks do not determine who we are. Misinformed stories created from hurt and pain only perpetuate the inevitable love-filled excursion to be had by all. The freedom within all poor choices is that we can choose again.

Our limitation is not a lacking of any physical feature or material presence. Our limitation lies in not believing we have everything we are yearning for, and what God activates in us is an ever-knowing need to come home.

Attached to too much and yet nothing at all robs us from the very truth of who we are and our purpose.

Walking away, letting go, and remembering are self-induced mechanisms for spiritual renewal with God. Our connection with this source of power is the missing link when we find ourselves lost in the forest of distraction, pressure, expectations, and the thrusting force of society's image.

God's gravity pulls us toward him as a means for staying in the vibrational vision of who we are. Knowing ourselves in this way contradicts the pull that society details within its conformity.

Much like watching a sporting event, which we all love to do, consciousness is having an awareness of the beliefs you hold, the people in your circle, and the events you take part in. It is an eye-watching occurrence of you and what you do every day. It is characterized by a reflective process of curiosity and plugging in to your roots. This high level of awareness cannot be stumbled upon. It requires mindful intent.

God's grace, his second chances, afford us purposeful renovation as a daily practice. "Ask and you shall receive" (Matthew 7:7 KJV) is the love language between God and his tribe.

The RETURNING

*What lies behind us and what lies before us are
tiny matters compared to what lies within us. To be
yourself in a world that is constantly trying to make
you something else is the greatest accomplishment.*
-Ralph Waldo Emerson

I learned to trust who I was and be who I was and love who I was.
The lessons will come, and I know who I am. I am love. I am worthy
of love. I am enough. I am.

⟜

Our life has the power to influence who we are, as well as the
power to guide us back to who we are when we have forgotten.
Living our truth and living authentically is a knowing that the distractions we encounter along our way, by way of people, events
and circumstances, are given to us as a means for learning—personal growth and development. Within each encounter is a free
will for how we will choose to view the learning. We always have
a choice to witness our life experiences as good and joyful, or

harmful and detrimental. We choose whether we believe learning to be an opportunity to grow, or an opportunity to wallow in self-pity. Growing is loving, and wallowing is fear-filled.

The unknown and the uncharted can be scary to our egoist mind's intent. It cannot be pursued alone or in isolation. We must rely upon God to build a union with us and travel in partnership toward the all-knowing world of love, compassion, and wholehearted interaction. *A Course in Miracles* reminds us that in this way, "Every interaction is a holy one." Every aspect of our human life has the capacity for learning and, if we are willing, has the unlimited potential to teach us to a higher level of living and a grander consciousness.

We are bound by a perceptive reality sequestered within our human mind. Our perception can predict faithfully or numb joyfully. In our daily dreamlike states, we can feel a way through our experiences based on truth and based on learning.

It is only our willingness to not be willing that lends us to altered states of being who we are. And in every present moment is a free will offering to choose again, start over, gain clarity, and be the difference.

~⌖~

the remembering —
being open to
the newness of life

What if?

This question of curious intent haunts my inner voice and the beating of my own heart.

What if this spiral staircase and the climbing of those steps toward my home, the me of who I am, was an illusion?

What if my inner warfare between the dueling ego and the soul was a bad dream?

What if the stories and the people who played the parts were acting out a true love affair?

What if love was always available, and I had just forgotten who I was?

Yes, it is the remembering. I had forgotten who I was.

The intimacy between my outer Self and my inner Self relied on a vulnerability that took courage. This courage, free of judgment and expectations, is not a destination. It is a love story. My willingness to choose being comfortable over being brave got lost in the swirling of life's quickness. My love story held different endings, and by my choices found me lost and alone. The collateral beauty is a love affair between our ego and our soul. It is our love story. It is who we are and how we live our life. It is the choices we make and our freewill to choose again.

God granted me the serenity of an awakening, a moment in time when my eyes became fully opened and my heart began to beat again to this newness. It was everything a remembering should entail—the lust for fresh ways that activated sensual and spiritual aspects of myself I had forgotten were within me, the glory for seeing the vibrancy of all I am, and the responsiveness of my surroundings to this newfound freedom. The freedom to be me in all ways and all times.

Kyle Gray—a psychic medium and an angel master—says, "The Divine waits gently in the heart of the warrior."

The heart of a warrior? I had never thought of a warrior as having a heart: only as having weaponry to battle. Maybe there is no battle between the ego and the soul. Maybe it is a love story—learning to bear witness to choosing love, learning to see what matters most and choosing that, learning to grow upward and onward from pain, learning to be oneself and loving that Self.

I had never thought of myself as a warrior, although many times I felt the urgency of battle and the efforts of a yearning to win. God waits for us to come back home to him and to our SELF. The Self is the one he created us to be. It is our true one. It is the goodness and the joyfulness of who we are. It is the ego as the powerhouse to be stronger and question our wrong moves and misled directions in life. The heart is the pathway for all that is, and all that is possible. It is the cross-section for the ego and the soul to come home together and collaborate in authenticity and truthfulness.

God's synchronistic endeavors were noticed one week when I kept hearing the word "warrior" and seeing it in content on my phone and in my emails, and hearing it on the radio. That was the week Kyle Gray's quote came upon my eyes. The same week I heard the song by Hannah Kerr titled, "Warrior". It replenished my new-found understanding for breathing; seeing the light within dark moments; learning as a way to build strength, faith and love as inner weapons; and a remembering that no one person, event or circumstance in my life was in vain. It was gifted to me as a means for learning to love.

Fear had trampled my heart, shoving love to an almost non-existent feature. My beliefs ran ragged through the storm of life's wild momentum. Unfortunate and negative wanderings with wrong choices, mistaken identity, and misrepresentation kept me chained to an alter ego. I knew something felt off, and I knew I was not me. I felt wildly lost within my own life.

My un-remembering was an unconscious choice and became my sole responsibility to recover that which was impressed upon me at birth, that beautiful day I entered this world filled with magic and pure essence of heart-pumping joy. The innocence of childhood and a sequestered upbringing landed me in an unconscious state of a dense outer reality. Just as the folding happened in perfect form, so did the unfolding.

A shift, a crack, an opening led me to a beginning, my beginning. This new start filled with such trepidation and anxiety brought nuggets of fascination and thrill. It was a vast learning with depth and light, shows of both dark and brightness. The learning, the lessons, the mountains of conversations were direct invites from God to come home. He yearned for me to return to who I was and come home to my heart as a daily ritual for living.

The choice to return was a gift I had to give myself as a token for all the joy and appreciation for each person, each event, each belief, and each excavation for recovering the truth, my truth.

The story of love within the boundaries of this journey is the awakening to the abundance of necessity for the ego and the soul to unite in efforts that far exceed the daily grind of an outer reality. These two entities can marry a pattern for collaborating and honoring the diversity each brings to our consciousness. They can work together for collateral beauty.

My ego and my soul must hold hands, skip through my life as one force for love, and honor the blessings each hold for surrendering my life, this life, to love. The ego serves as a task master intently eye-balling the outcomes. She comes from me to help me pay attention and convert my fear and worry and doubt and anger to a more useful way. My soul, quietly existing, knows my heart and sends rippling messages of love. She gracefully reminds me of the immense abundance within the world.

They must work together—see each other, hear each other, and belong to each other. One cannot survive nor thrive without the other. Their union, within the heart, serves as a North Star symbolic of a ring used in marriage. For better or for worse, the ego and the soul are divinely intertwined.

A Course in Miracles states, "What you think you are is a belief to be undone."

My ego showed me those beliefs early on in my life, and like any dutiful soldier I held tightly to them. I, in no way, wanted to lose the battle. This love story was the undoing of my beliefs.

God, the force for love, pulled me through each experience. The scars and the painful memories serve only as anecdotes to document the journey to return. Within each one, finding my strength to learn required effort. Pema Chodron notes, "When we protect ourselves so we won't feel pain, that protection becomes like armor, like armor that imprisons the softness of the heart."

My earlier acquisitions imprisoned me. I faithfully walked this battlefield using the armor as a shield and as an accessory. Proud of that metal hardness to my heart, thinking I won the battle often found me shameful for losing me on the battlefield of life.

Surrendering myself to the uncharted found me learning a more resourceful and loving way to live life married to my ego and my soul in union.

The 90-second rule I had learned from Pema Chodron offered me the courage and bravery to share a seat with each painful, disturbing, and confused emotion. The fear that such emotions often render gave way to a hope that included no judgment or definition. And as promised, they would disappear. I had not sat with any of the painful experiences of my past. Instead, I had allowed a circuit of storytelling to run continually through my head and charge quickly in opposite direction of the pain that came from an organic life. We are not meant to escape painful moments. This continual escape and running away programmed new systems only to be deleted, and the old ones to maintain their positions as triggers for me.

One day I ended up in a Kundalini yoga class with Siri Atma Kaur: I was scared, lost, and unknown. As Siri Atma pushed a button that exalted a song, I completely unraveled on that mat. The words gripped my heart as the waterworks flooded my sight. Tina Malia's words softly enlightened my heart to my own love story, "*This is the sound of one heart starting to hear; this is the sound of faith stepping out of fear; the journey of one soul's passage through time; and this is one lone dreamer learning to fly."*

I felt myself on this life path stumbling through a deep fog and working to make sense of my past and my now. As the words rained over my heart that day, I knew my soul was transforming, and I knew I was eroding my fears. All I had operated from was fear. Sometimes it was disguised as love because it was given to those I deeply cared for, such as my family, my friends, and my peers. My fear was hidden amongst the masks I learned to wear. The roles I played on the stage of my life scripted my every move.

That day, on the mat in the Kundalini class, was the plugging in of the ever-so-tiny light coming to its brightness deep inside the depths of my caves of past experiences and the choices of a mistaken identity.

The light came with a voice inviting me, and as I laid on that mat, I knew my life was forever changing, transforming, converting, and evolving. Malia's words, *"And your love is shining; in everything I do; and I hear you calling for me; for all roads lead to you,"* rang in my heart. They spoke to me loud and clear. They reminded me of my yearning to come home. To find myself amidst the rubble of my past assumptions, to know me from the excavation of who I really am as one who kept moving onward when life's stormy moments hit hard, and to receive the joyous gifts within the blessings of a well-lived life.

The voice? It was my soul that had been living dormant for so many years. It was my soul beginning to come alive as we, the ego in attendance, were returning home.

Today, as I sit on my mat in another Kundalini class led by Siri Atma Kaur, I find myself crying again. This time is different. These are tears of joy because I have come home.

As the music played and my body did the job of tuning in, I remembered who I am. The reminder played within the melody of the song, the wisdom, the truth, and leaving the darkness behind. Choosing to see the light within every experience as one who has led me here.

My ego and my soul gently caress the longing of my heart to be love, to see love, and to hear love. My ultimate free will making the decision each moment gifted to me, to come home. The freedom of me breathes in all possibilities and sends the energy of that air back out to the world, rippling toward all who need to discover who they are.

I am home.

My ego and my soul spiraling in succession in a rhythmic melody of love. My heart captures the remnants of my past as FULL-filled consciousness. I awaken to the universal truth that God has called me, and I have come home to who I am.

I am home. I am.

Index

H

healing 73, 74

heart v, ix, x, xi, xii, xiii, xiv, xv, xvi, xvii, xviii, 5, 6, 7, 9, 10, 11, 16, 17, 18, 23, 24, 27, 28, 29, 39, 40, 41, 42, 43, 44, 45, 47, 53, 54, 56, 57, 62, 63, 65, 66, 71, 72, 74, 75, 77, 78, 82, 83, 85, 89, 90, 97, 98, 107, 108, 109, 110, 111, 112, 113

Holy Spirit ix, xvi, xvii, xviii

I

identity vii, xviii, 37, 41, 43, 47, 83, 84, 90, 109, 112

inner dialogues 12, 78

impression, the 17-18

inspiration xvi

intimacy 27, 107

intuitive ix

J

Jesus ix, xvi, 84

journey i, viii, xi, xviii, 5, 14, 16, 17, 42, 45, 78, 85, 91, 100, 110, 112

joy xi, xiii, 10, 27, 42, 45, 74, 77, 84, 90, 92, 100, 109, 113

K

KJV (King James Version Bible) 101

Kundalini 111, 112, 113

L

Leaf, Dr. Caroline 56

learning ix, xv, xviii, 41, 42, 47, 48, 71, 72, 75, 78, 81, 82, 83, 84, 86, 98, 99, 100, 103, 104, 108, 109, 111, 112

trust 13, 23, 34, 66, 75, 83, 103

truth i, ii, iii, 11, 15, 33, 39, 40, 43, 45, 61, 64, 66, 67, 78, 98, 101, 103, 104, 109, 113

U

uncharted xi, 104, 111

unconditional love 73

Universe ix, xiii, xiv, 73, 99

V

vulnerability 107

W

warrior 109

wholeheartedness xv, 57

wisdom v, 8, 9, 11, 42, 83, 86, 113

worthiness 6, 13, 99

Book Club Questions

inspired from the beginning

1. My heart marks always aided in shifting my perspective in any moment.

   What sign or symbol do you know brings you home to who you are? (AND...if you are not aware, pay attention... you will begin to see)

blind-sided

2. Our life is our classroom. The learning—the growth endurances—is our curriculum. Name a learning you have had recently. How did it change you for the better? What did you keep? What did you leave behind?

3. Letting go and getting still are tools for a life in joy. How have these served you well?

4. What is your trend—to sit with an emotion in stillness or react? (A reaction is how you respond outward. This could be talking about it to everyone, yelling at others, social media posting, shopping, eating, drinking, etc.) What could be a benefit of non-reacting?

5. Going inward is a mechanism for non-reaction. How have you gone inward and found wisdom?

impressions

6. Who are you? Who are you not?

   These sound so simple, and yet we create dilemmas around the self-serving response to each. Discover these answers and you have won. Love wins!

our mirror

7. Our stories are held deep within our minds and bodies. Share a story that typically unfolds in your head. How might you retell that story?

8. We hold our sacredness in our Pandora's box. What are you holding in your sacred box deep within your heart? Set it free so it has less power over you.

9. As women, we measure our worth according to our physical features. What are other, more loving, ways to measure our worth? These actually matter!

love defined

10. "Hopeful took my heart away." Love is a choice.

    Share about a time when you chose love. Be mindful of this moment always.

11. "I stared at them in awe of their reverence for the unemotional."

    How can seeing and hearing help us understand more?

12. We play many roles in our life. Some are driven from a sense of self and others are hiding mechanisms.

    What might be the impact of this dual nature of existing? How can we live more authentically?

going and gone

13. We hold constructs (a belief or thought pattern) that many times are not healthy or productive. What is your most influential construct and how did you acquire such thinking?

reckless revelations

14. What sacred rituals do you hold in your heart?

15. Shadow beliefs are often misunderstood systems of thinking we hold as truth. How can we honor the shadow *and* believe again in a more loving manner?

16. Tell about a time when you were lost. How did you find your way back?

the dwelling

17. What is your curriculum? What are you learning? Learning is how we grow. The vastness of this movement is dependent upon our willingness to open our hearts, our minds, and our bodies to gain the significance and release the unimportant. Joy is knowing we are always expanding.

losing

18. "Laughter was our medicine." What moments bring you laughter? How might you receive more laughter in your life?

19. Aha moments are precious experiences that bring us to our awakening. They are "a bolt of fresh air in our heart." What has been your most loving aha moment? Let this be your daily mantra.

20. "Freedom is only found in the present moment." How is this true for you?

in the present

21. "…it's that feeling of uncertainty that can completely put you in chains of fear at times." What leads us to this chaining process? Why might we choose this way of coping? How can we change it?

22. How do you focus on what matters? What factors often distract you?

23. Have you ever found yourself at a "rusted intersection"? What wisdom did it reveal?

changing locations

24. What are your sources of energy? Are these sustainable?

25. How have you escaped a no-win situation?

26. "Prayer is a continual chain linked together with gratitude, surrendering, and stillness." Prayer can take on many forms. What is your most treasured form of prayer?

renovation

27. Building blocks are the foundation for sustainability. What are your most loving and productive building blocks? How do you sustain them?

walking away

28. In what capacity do you serve others? Describe how it fills you with joy.

29. The voice heard in our moments of stillness is our own heart and soul speaking to us. In what ways do you honor and listen to this voice of yours? How do you teach with your voice?

30. Our bodies are our signals showing us the way home to who we are. How does your body signal to you?

the clearing

31. Getting rid of stuff frees up space for what really matters. What stuff do you collect? How does it serve its purpose? How is getting rid of stuff like letting go of control?

32. Stillness and laughter are medicine for the soul. How is this true for you?

the attack

33. Describe a time when you belonged to a group and a projection of a raw emotion sent you away?

34. Love is always available. How do you remove the barriers in your life so you can love for real?

35. "You are stronger than you think." How is this true for you?

the remembering

36. Which comes first as one who is awakened—vulnerability or courage?

37. Can we be comfortable and brave at the same time? Describe how this might look in our everyday lives.

38. What are the synchronistic patterns in your life that seem to lead you home to who you are?

New Book Coming Soon!

Welcome In:
An Illumination of Self

*Cultivating a
Sacredness Within*

Kristi Peck

Introducing
a New Way

Looking up and out, how can we not respect this
ever-vigilant cognizance that distinguishes us:
the capability to envision, to dream, and to invent?
the ability to ponder ourselves? and be aware of
our existence on the outer arm of a spiral galaxy
in an immeasurable ocean of stars?
Cognizance is our crest.
Vanna Bonta

Spiraling.

In a roundabout manner, I am spiraling.

As I stand here, at home, in my humanness, I look outward. No this is not it. I do not see what I want to see. I am not in comfort here. I am in un-rest here looking outward.

How can that be?

What I see is fear, and it frightens me. My skin crawls up and down my physical-ness. Breathing is hard to grasp. I search for the warmth and miss the target.

Sure, I witness kind acts of humans doing for each other. Sure, I witness humans helping each other. Sure, I witness the regeneration of natural tendencies.

These outward projections do not satisfy me. I am searching and spiraling. I want more.

The revolving motion back and forth as I move. But, in what direction am I moving? My spiral flow is somewhat lost.

I have always thought I had to move up. That's what I was taught to believe. Yes! Up and out are forward moving. Or, so I thought. Success was definitive once you moved up the ladder, up the pay scale, up the road, or up in rank.

These outward projections seemed to leave me barren and stiff. I could not find myself in the movement of them. They always left me wanting more. Moving up as a way to accomplish was not satisfaction.

Expansion. The theme of getting wider, covering more ground, staying who I am and getting bigger. Expanding found me enveloped in the warmth and comfort of a loving space. There was a fullness and a sacredness in this flow of expansion.

In this awakened moment, a force nudges my heart. An ever-knowing that the outward projection is not the truth, the way, or the life. It is non-sustaining in a fast paced and always on the go human world.

I had forgotten. I had gotten it misunderstood.

Spiraling.

The way we journey in our human form derives from a loving entity hypnotized from our core. The spiral of life symbolizes our journey as an awakened consciousness. Our beginning derives from a core within us. This core committed to upon birth and yet forgotten along the journey.

I am this core and I am a forgotten one. As a realization of my coming home, I must now learn again to live within the means of my core. This core is a heartfelt sacredness that allows me to reach out to the far corners of earth as an expanded one. With love governing all that we are, we can live our most authentic lives from a power and an all-knowing that beyond the extraterrestrial existence of the earthly inhabitants, we are love. Everything we do, can do, and must do, flows from this foundational source.

According to Carl Jung, the Swiss psychiatrist who founded analytical psychology, "The spiral is an archetypal symbol that represents cosmic force."

Who we are, the core of our being, is birthed cosmically upon our arrival on this earthly plane. It is a force that will pull, or push, us into the fullness of the truth. We can be distracted from the truth. We can have forgotten the truth. We can hide from the truth. And the truth, being a force of the universe, will always yield us back to our home.

"Home is where the heart is." (Erasure)

In essence, coming home to who we are is a cosmic intention to keep us grounded and in the fullness of a well-lived life.

But, once we have forgotten, gotten distracted, and possibly even hidden from that truth of who we are, we must awaken to it. Upon awakening to the newness of our home, the heart of who we are, we then welcome in the presence of this cosmic operation.

We open the door to a new way, to more love, and to a sacredness like no other. In honor and reverence for the blessing bestowed upon us, we must illuminate who we are so the world can see the love within us. We must welcome in our illuminated self and exercise a sacredness daily.

Our journey continues, in that spiral motion, as we continue learning in expanded ways. Love is the constant that flows effortlessly within the confines of the spiral motion. Like a thread, it is quietly and softly aligning all that is sacred in place and with reverence.

The journey continues spiraling. In the silence of an awakening, the gentle yearning to understand the misunderstood through restoration of what was left. It is an honor deserving full resolve and a graceful charge to release what was being held captive in the heart for too long.

The journey continues spiraling. The slow process of unfolding the unions forever bonded and wiping away that which suffocates and barricades the beating of the human heart. This allows God to enter the agreement—we are here to be.

No more outward searching. Desire must be gathered from within. Hope must be blossomed from within. Fear must be set aside. From the core of our heart, we must live within our illuminated self and welcome in an enlightened way of living.

The SHADOW Seen

"Transit umbra; lux permanent"
(Translation: The shadow passes; the light remains)

The sun shines brightly—light exudes from a ball of fire while illuminating a glow of orange, yellow, and a slight greenish blue. It is our forever form of radiance as it warms, it electrifies, and it embodies oneness. Light blazes within each of us effortlessly bringing about our unique gifts laid upon this Earth. This light is our essence. It governs how we walk, talk, and love. Our light never dims and never leaves.

Only when we willingly allow another person or circumstance to shield our light, does it go void. Void by way of what stands in the way.

The shadow, while creating a darkened effect, serves to pause the light. In this reflective state, one creates a sacred space for connection to the remembering and the all-knowing. Only love is real, and anything outside of that is an illusion and a disconnection. The shadow is not a forever accessory.

A light, our light, is a forever possibility. As the shadows move past us, we illuminate the essence of our heartfelt self. And, in the moment this miracle occurs, love wins.

─◦─

The phone call came.

I've been here before. The familiarity of the words being said, the circumstance unfolding, and the emotions erupting from within my shell. I am remembering well the vividness of such an experience.

The experience, once before, had opened up a pathway for love to enter where I had blocked and barricaded. It gave breath to a suffocation. It gave connection to a disconnected soul. It brought together a union of two life forms. The marriage of dark and light in a never-ending tale for truth and the way for a well-lived life.

As I answered that call, something in me remembered. With hesitation, my heart slowed to a snail's pace. In my recall, it became apparent that my body remembered it all too well. The uncontrollable spasm of the unknown and the fright. The blood pumping with a viciousness of desperation to escape. My head lifting and floating like a hot air balloon on a cool day.

What's happening?

I know. I remember. I have been here before.

My child has accepted another role to be my teacher. With the grace of God at our fingertips, we relinquish control and adversely welcome another moment. In this moment, we shall go deeper in our learning. Me as the student and the child as the teacher.

A Course in Miracles says, "When the student is ready, the teacher appears."

An awakening is a new day and a new opportunity to choose again. It brings forth a sacredness of space that holds the availability to renew with freshness, reframe with depth of character, and a recharge of energetic systems. My awakening is my ready moment, the start of my again.

As my body responds to the fright received in that phone call of trouble, something seems a bit off. There is a strange and unrecognizable force swirling within my heart. My heart slowing down and speaking loud and clear with such clarity of vision. The whirlwind of a spiral pulls me away from the dark that seemed inevitable and gently pushes me toward a softness.

"This is not you," it whispers.

I hear it. In this moment, I hear it. This force within is intense. My heart beats a bit smoother.

It goes on, "It is not him."

I hear it too. My heart quickly finds its rhythm again, a bit faster and yet still slow. It's a calming melody.

My consciousness elevates to the top of the mountain peering over. I see me. I see him. We are called for more learning. This is our sacred curriculum. As teacher and as student, we will thrive to new levels, to deeper understanding, and to the cosmic foundation of pure love.

The child cannot fathom how the trouble happened. He had been following all the rules life placed on him in his earthly school. He had been paying attention to what was being said to him by his teachers. There is a sadness enveloping him, a glow that appears dimmer at first glance.

As a mother, I worry and I fear. I see him. I have always seen him. This episode is not him. It is just a lesson to be learned. I must rise to the podium to speak with clarity to him. He needs to hear my love and my heartfelt vision.

In this minuscule of a moment in time, I have the power to teach, to inspire, and to change his world. I am scared, and yet I know the words I will present will be monumental to his call to action. This monumental moment holds a sacredness for both of us. I know my role as his mom, his teacher, and his student. My consciousness rises to a new level. There is no shame for this trouble we are in. There is no blame for this trouble we are in. There is no anger for the detour on our journey. There is only love in this moment.

The present moment holds everything we want. It expands our desires and uploads our wishes. Our curriculum between parent and child is learning and loving. The remembering is a powerful force guiding me to open the door to this moment, this opportunity, and welcome in an illumination of who I am.

God is here. I feel his warmth of comfort, I hear his voice telling me all will be well, and I know in my heart we are expanding in our curriculum called life.

There are choices in this present moment. So many choices to be had, and my heart knows only one way will lead us back home to the heart of who we are. The parent and the child in the present moment have options. I know this, and I want love to be the thread that spirals within us as we live well. In this shadowed moment, I choose love again.

The child is everything I am and everything I am not. I see him. I know this moment of learning requires me to let go and give God the reigns. He will give me the words to say. He lights our way when we find ourselves shadowed.

The present moment is a nugget of time. It has a clear beginning and a virtuous ending. Within that ever-tiny length of clock-ticking everything, we always have the world—all that is needed, wanted, and loved.

The present moment requires all of the oneness within us that exists. Our eyes must see. Our ears must listen. Our mind must know. Our hands must hold. Our mouth must find stillness. We must be ever in that moment. Not back in time nor pushed ahead of it.

I was learning of the power within those present moment nuggets. They were gems often beginning from a rocky and rushed sense of expectation. They were priceless guarantees that life is always unfolding and spiraling around sparklers of learning and unlearning, holding on and letting go, fear and love, and trusting beyond all measure.

The shadow moved in. I remembered this space. I stepped back in time to recall the details of a past only to discover it really did not exist. The past remembrance was an illusion. In the dark shadowy space of breathing in and out, and uncharted newness from the core of who I am, I welcomed in another way to honor the teacher, the student, God, and the moment we were gifted.

I took my fear, my trepidation, and my worry, and I laid them aside. I offered them to God on a silver platter because my heart spoke and assured me He had a plan bigger than I understood. His plan was bigger and better than anything I could ever have imagined. He knew what we needed and what our desire wanted. His power could make anyone and anything walk on water. And that he did.

So, out of the rubble of a torn down past, our newness had risen. We began to operate from a different energy source. We saw past the outside existence and keened in to God's never-ending supply of grace and love.

It charged our batteries for the long haul. Choosing to give God our fear, our doubt, our worry allowed us to have what was left. And we decided to love what was left. That was pure joy, love-filled happiness and laughter, and a continued classroom of learning.

We, as parents, are both teacher and student. The child is always the student and the teacher. The interwoven capacity for each to move as needed is a means of serving God's higher vision for our sacred relationship. It is what governs our ultimate purpose.

That day, the child entered the role of teacher, and the parent learned. I learned to love more deeply, to trust more, and to surrender more purposefully. I learned to honor the present moment in reverence to God's love. I learned to be willing to not know, not control, and not project the dark emotions that arise from an unexpected event that hurts. I learned to find joy when I give God all the other that shadows it.

That day, the parent entered the role of teacher, and the child learned. The child learned to trust in his fortitude, to love more willingly, and to be guided by a mission. The child learned a better way of becoming. The child learned that conditions change and love always remains. The child found himself amidst the rubble of a shadowy decision and found his light that had dimmed.

That present moment, the parent and the child accepted the invitation God granted and transformed a storm into beauty. They owned the responsible growth and endurance. They choose love.

And in the end, the brightness returned.

About the Author

Kristi Peck is a Spiritual Teacher and Intuitive. She has been teaching for 25 years in many capacities. In addition, she is a writer and an honest storyteller. Her stories and her wisdom captivate listeners and allow for the authenticity of each individual to flourish. Whether it's an audience or a client, she'll have you thinking hard and laughing as she uses her intuition to guide learning for those seeking understanding from everyday experiences and challenges. Kristi offers perspective, compassion and a loving spirit as she inspires others to choose love in all ways that matter.

Kristi's warmth and vulnerability as she shares her journey of self-discovery will enable you to awaken your truth, open your heart and begin your own journey. Her deep connection with spirit and her ability to communicate with loved ones in the afterlife are additional gifts she offers to her clients.

You can find her laughing with friends and family, reading, shopping or watching movies…always with her favorite cup of coffee in hand.

Kristi lives in St. Louis, Missouri with her husband and their four children. She is devoted to leading a love-inspired life by example.

Connect with Kristi online at her website www.kristipeck.com